THE SEA & OTHER POEMS

(La Mer & Autres Poèmes)

TITLES from BLACK WIDOW PRESS

TRANSLATION SERIES

Chanson Dada: Selected Poems by Tristan Tzara
translated & edited by Lee Harwood

Approximate Man & Other Writings by Tristan Tzara
translated & edited by Mary Ann Caws

Poems of Andre Breton: A Bilingual Anthology
translated & edited by by Jean-Pierre Cauvin and Mary Ann Caws

Last Love Poems of Paul Eluard
translated with an introduction by Marilyn Kallet

Capital of Pain by Paul Eluard
translated by Mary Ann Caws, Patricia Terry, and Nancy Kline

Love, Poetry (L'amour la poésie) by Paul Eluard
translated with an introduction by Stuart Kendall

The Sea & Other Poems by Guillevic
translated by Patricia Terry
with an introduction by Monique Chefdor

Essential Poems & Writings of Robert Desnos: A Bilingual Anthology
edited with an introduction and essay by Mary Ann Caws
(forthcoming)

Essential Poems & Writings of Joyce Mansour: A Bilingual Anthology
translated with an introduction by Serge Gavronsky
(forthcoming)

Eyeseas (Les Ziaux) by Raymond Queneau
translated with an introduction by Daniela Hurezanu & Stephen Kessler
(forthcoming)

Poems of A. O. Barnabooth by Valery Larbaud
translated with an introduction by Ron Padgett and Bill Zavatsky
(forthcoming)

MODERN POETRY SERIES

An Alchemist with One Eye on Fire
Clayton Eshleman

Archaic Design
Clayton Eshleman
(forthcoming)

Backscatter
John Olson
(forthcoming)

NEW POET SERIES

Signal from Draco: Poems of Mebane Robertson
(forthcoming)

www.blackwidowpress.com

The Sea & Other Poems

(La Mer & Autres Poèmes)

GUILLEVIC

translated by
PATRICIA TERRY
with an introduction by
MONIQUE CHEFDOR
and a foreword by
LUCIE ALBERTINI GUILLEVIC

BLACK WIDOW PRESS
Boston, Mass.

THE SEA & OTHER POEMS
Guillevic

Black Widow Press edition, June 2007

Black Widow Press is an imprint of Commonwealth Books, Inc., Boston.
Joseph S. Phillips, Publisher.

All Black Widow Press books are printed on acid-free paper and put into sewn and glued bindings

Black Widow Press
www.blackwidowpress.com

ISBN-13: 978-0-97684498-3
ISBN-10: 0-97684498-2

Library of Congress Cataloging-in-Publication Data

Guillevic, Eugène, 1907-1997.
[Selections. English & French. 2007]
The sea & other poems = La mer & autres poèmes / Guillevic ; translated by Patricia Terry ; with a foreword by Lucie Albertini Guillevic ; and, an introduction by Monique Chefdor.
p. cm.
ISBN 978-0-9768449-8-3
1. Guillevic, Eugène, 1907–1997—Translations into English. I. Terry, Patricia Ann, 1929– II. Title. III. Title: Sea and other poems. IV. Title: Mer & autres poèmes. V. Title: Mer et autres poèmes.

PQ2613.U46A2 2007
841'.912—dc22

2007017699

Prepress production by Windhaven Press (www.windhaven.com)
Printed by Thomson-Shore
Printed in the United States

10 9 8 7 6 5 4 3 2 1

Contents

THE SEA & OTHER POEMS

(La Mer & Autres Poèmes)

Foreword

The appearance in 2007 of this new bilingual collection of Guillevic's poems published in the distinguished Black Widow Press modern poetry series fills me with joy and gratitude.

Joy because any new translation is to be greeted like a new birth, like a surprising shaft of light and hope, a precious opening.

Gratitude because Guillevic often said that the translation of poems was not difficult but simply impossible. Human beings, however, he used to add, have only succeeded in achieving the impossible (transmitting sound and images over long distances, walking on the moon) and failed to accomplish the possible (putting an end to famine in the world and to wars).[1] And I truly believe that the impossible is offered us here: so much talent, intelligence, attention, and sensitivity have been expended to produce this book.

Patricia Terry and Monique Chefdor have worked in remarkable harmony and with complete respect for the text.

Yes, we all know that to translate a poem is to dedicate oneself to the "re-creation" of another poem, another because, of course, it is in another language. And, for Guillevic, a disciple of Hölderlin, "to succeed in the making of the poem" required capturing its unique quality and the "sacredness lying in its heart." It meant "introducing the reader into the temple which the poem is and allowing him to attend and participate in the rites

1 *Vivre en poésie,* p.155.

celebrated there."[2] Truly an impossible task, but not for someone who is a poet, who has the gift of transmitting, of passing poetry on, selecting the elements of the poem which are transportable, transposable. That is the true mission of the poet-translator. That is what Patricia Terry offers us.

Guillevic also wrote, "Poor poetry translators, blessed poetry translators, torn from one dilemma to the next, dissatisfied, displeased with themselves, only sustained by their questioning, blessed nevertheless, in the glory they bestow upon themselves through the service they render to poetry."[3]

Poetry, that "colossal adventure," that "something else" which nurtures the child still to be born within all of us, and which ceaselessly keeps vigil in every heart.

I wish you a good and attentive reading, with my thanks.

Lucie Guillevic Albertini
Paris, december 30, 2006.
(translated by Monique Chefdor)

---

2 *Colloquium Helveticum : traduire la poésie,* Peter Lang, Bern, Frankfurt am Main, New York, 1986.

3 *Vivre en poésie.*

Guillevic

Or

A wink at indeterminate matter.

Le poème Est chaque fois, Toujours,	The poem is, Every time, Always,
La première aventure La dernière, la seule,	The first adventure, The ultimate one, the only one,
Où tout se joue, Où tout se donne.	When everything is at stake, When everything is offered.

Inclus, p.227.

Widely recognized in France and throughout the world, Guillevic's works span the entire second half of the XXth century, from 1942 when Gallimard published the ground-breaking *Terraqué,* considered by many as the matrix of his work, through the XXIst century with Gallimard recently publishing several posthumous volumes. One of the most significant and original voices in contemporary poetry, Guillevic has been translated into more than fifty languages in sixty countries. There are, to date, 150 limited editions of his poems illustrated by renowned artists including: Dubuffet, Manessier, Léger, Debré, Baltazar, Cortot, Dorny, Pouperon, and others. Many of his works have been set to music, and interest among composers is increasing. Numerous radio and television interviews as well as publications attest to the very personal quality of interest both his writings and his personality invite.

The recipient of many literary prizes and distinctions in France and abroad[1] during his lifetime, in 2007, on the occasion of the hundredth anniversary of his birth, Guillevic has been nominated by the French Board of Culture and Communications for inclusion in the highly selective "Célébrations Nationales" as one of the writers and artists to be honored.[2]

Guillevic, nevertheless, stands out as a singularly independent figure in his century. A contemporary of the Surrealists, a close friend of Eluard and Aragon, he was never enthusiastic about Surrealism. In *Vivre en Poésie*, (Living in Poetry), a book length interview which amounts to an autobiography, he recalls returning Breton's *Manifestoes of Surrealism* to his philosophy teacher with the dismissive comment: "I don't see what it adds to Rimbaud except a more academic version."[3] Later on in the same series of dialogues, he declares: "The important movement of the first quarter of the century was Dadaism."[4]

Like Jean Follain, whose influence he often acknowledged, he stood apart from all literary schools and movements of the time. In the thirties, thanks to Follain,[5] he began publishing in poetry reviews, but he owes his first major publication *Terraqué* to Marcel Arland who introduced him to Gallimard. Drieu la Rochelle, whom Guillevic held in great esteem despite

1 See attached chronology.

2 *Célébrations Nationales 2007*, Ministère de la Culture et de la Communication, Direction des Archives de France, Paris, 2006, p. 114–115 & 267-68.

3 *Vivre en Poésie, Entretiens avec Lucie Albertini Guillevic et Alain Vircondelet,* Paris, Stock, 1980, p.49.

4 ibid. p.100.

5 The booklet *Guillevic avec Jean Follain*, in collaboration with Lucie Albertini Guillevic, Collection &, PAB, Pully, Switzerland, 1993, gives a most moving and detailed account of the two poets' relationship.

their utterly divergent political viewpoints, helped considerably. At the same time, Guillevic befriended Valéry and also recognized that "Reverdy, Supervielle, and Milosz most influenced him."[6]

Guillevic lived in poetry as one lives in religion. Yet he was the very opposite of an ivory tower recluse. Deeply committed to social and civic causes, he had a full time career in State administration beginning as a deputy clerk in the local treasury office in Huningue, a little French town near Basel. Promoted to the Ministry of Finance and Economic Affairs in Paris in 1935, he became National Economy Inspector at the Ministry of Finance in Paris in 1946, a position he held until his retirement in 1967. One of his major responsiblities in that position was the coordination of development in northern Africa. Over and beyond his career as a civil servant, his dedication to the juridical and social rights of writers, his constant willingness to travel throughout the world in support of events on behalf of poetry (although he hated travelling),[7] his revival of the Mallarmé society which he presided for 18 years, and so many other functions he assumed without ever sparing himself, attest to his primordial dedication to poetry. Guillevic's innermost being and true life resided in poetry.

. . .	
Ne me demandez pas	Don't ask me
Ce qu'est le centre.	What is the center.
De cela je ne sais rien,	I know nothing about it,
Je sais seulement le retrouver	I only know how to find it again
Grâce à la poésie.	Thanks to poetry
. . .	

10/03/95
Quotidiennes, (2002)

---

6 *Vivre en Poésie,* p.101.
7 Two of his lecture tours were given in American and Canadian universities.

He always knew he wanted to be a poet. When he was only eight, he started writing poems in the manner of La Fontaine. Brought up by an unusually cruel mother[8] and a somewhat distant father in rather poor circumstances with few books at home, he discovered the power of the word in the psalms he used to sing as a choir boy at church. There was also a Holy Story book given to him by nursing sisters from a local hospital: "The world took another dimension. I learned the meaning of the epic."[9] At school, he discovered his masters, Lamartine, then Baudelaire and Rimbaud without ever forgetting his first discovery of La Fontaine to whom he dedicated *Art Poétique* (1989). Fluent in German, which he had to learn in Alsace, he was also deeply influenced by the German Romantics: Novalis, Hölderlin, and Heine whom he translated into French. Equally influential were Rilke and Expressionists like Trakl whom he also translated and to whom he felt much akin despite their many differences.[10]

His dedication to poetry, however, has much deeper roots. Guillevic indeed represents a rare blend of the pre-celtic, the Heraclitean and the post-quantum theory approaches to the world's enigma. In every interview[11] he would recall that he took his first steps among the megalithic standing stones of Carnac, the most ancient in the world, older than 5000 BC, and possibly even more ancient according to recent research. Although he left Carnac when he was two years old, he returned regularly through his early adolescent years. The mysterious silence of these pre-celtic monuments stamped him forever, imparting to him the injunction to find out the mystery of inert matter and the unknown language of those who aligned the stones. Throughout his poetry there are reminders of this fundamental imperative:

---

8 Hence the use of his sole patronym for the signature of all his publications. The suffering he endured was such that he rejected his first name for public use. Only much later his wife reconciled him with it in private life.

9 *Vivre en poésie*, p.44

10 *Florilèges*, PAB, Pully, Switzerland, 1993, gives a significant sampling of Guillevic's translations from German poetry.

11 See the bibliography for their listing.

Il y avait donc	So there was,
L'appel de Carnac.	The call of Carnac.
Comment chantaient-ils,	How did they sing,
Ceux des menhirs?	The people of the Menhirs?

Carnac, 1961, p.178.

Tout vient d'ailleurs,	Everything comes from elsewhere,
De plus ancien que lui,	Older,
De plus enraciné,	More deeply rooted,
Apporte les étapes,	Bringing with it the stages on its way,
L'origine parfois.	Sometimes the origin.

Inclus, 1973, p.54.

And this significant declaration:

"If I were born elsewhere than in Carnac, I don't know whether I would be different, but, all the same, it seems to me . . . that being born in a sacred land, it affects you."[12]

Affect him, it did. Although, at the time of the Spanish Civil War, Guillevic rejected the catholic church in which he had been brought up and entered the Communist party during the war when it was still clandestine, he never lost touch with a basic sense of the sacred which, for him, is the root of all poetry and life in general. In one of the very last interviews he gave two years before his death, he significantly sums up his quest:

"I would like to be able to think that I have succeeded in creating a poetic universe in which the practice of the sacred is a requirement of daily life."[13]

---

[12] *Vivre en poésie*, p.52.

[13] in *Tempête sous un crâne*, No 8, Rennes, 1995.

Such a statement points to the very core of Guillevic's goal in poetry. Because of his passion for the life of matter, his tendency to treat beings and things as equals, he has often been categorised as a materialist. At times he has even been called a "materialist mystic." In fact, there is hardly anything more inappropriate to Guillevic's inner experience. For him the dichotomy matter/spirit does not exist. The sense of the sacred in all things independent of an anthropomorphic divinity pervades the celtic and pre-celtic traditions. But Guillevic's attempt at summing up the world through poetry, harkens back to the pre-socratic search for unity in diversity.

Like Anaxagoras, Guillevic is fundamentally convinced, if not of a profound identity among the constituents of all forms of existence, at least, of an unknown but real unity to be grasped beyond the infinite levels of diversity experienced by sensory knowledge. For him the resolution of opposites, so much advocated by the Surrealists, is not a theoretical standpoint but a concrete experience of oneness with any form of existence. This is very much akin to Heraclitus's belief in an invisible harmony more beautiful than the visible.

Si je n'avais pas vécu	If I had not lived
Dans le calice des fleurs,	Inside the calyx of flowers
Autre serait le ciel	The sky would not be what it is.

Requis (1981), p.174.

And even more explicitly:

Il faudrait voir plus clair	We need to see more clearly
Pour voir tous les objets	In order to see all the objects
Comme entre eux ils se voient.	As they see each other.

Exécutoire, (1947), p.194.

Such reminders of pre-socratic aphorisms come even closer to the investigations of contemporary science whose findings increasingly abolish the polarity observed/observer just as Guillevic's poetry does, the world being perceived as a system of inseparable interacting and ever moving components for which sheer conceptual thinking cannot fully account. With both Heraclitus and post-quantum theory, Guillevic shares an acute awareness of the fleeting ever elusive character of any grasp on the ultimate. His own words clearly acknowledge such kinship:

"What matters to me in this world, is to try and see what it really is, and what we really are, what we are in relationship to things, in relationship to ourselves . . . The poet is less a seer than an observer (voyant/ voyeur), and here I refer to pre-socratic poetry when a poet was at once and the same time a scholar, a thinker and a bard. When I hear some scientists today, I feel such a synthesis will not be impossible for ever."[14]

Analogies with Eastern philosophy will naturally come to mind. In my opinion, however, utmost caution should be used in attempting to assimilate Guillevic's lapidary style and "inside/outside" perception of all forms of reality with Zen or Tibetan Buddhism or Hindu scriptures. The coincidence is a matter of innate perception, not the conscious expression of an adhesion to any spiritual tradition in particular. It is a fact, nevertheless, that many of Guillevic's poems do arrest the mind in the same manner as oriental words of wisdom do. The reader experiences a shock of recognition, indicating, but not revealing, a mystery at the heart of the misleadingly obvious. There may lie the essence of Guillevic's humor. As Lucie Albertini puts it so simply and therefore so powerfully in her preface to *Present* from which we offer several excerpts, the deepest revelations can be conveyed through the incongruous.

Guillevic's poetry is the opposite of the hermetic. His apparent simplicity, however, is the result of a ceaseless probing into the inner being of things in order to elucidate the identity of all identities and give it a concrete tangible

---

[14] *Vivre en poésie*, p. 175.

reality. This is why, even when he evokes his birthplace, the source of the major themes of his work, he never actually describes. Instead, he captures the essence of the place or the object, the sea, the rock, the lake, the moor etc. He never writes the self observing, nor the world observed, but attempts to restore individuality to things, thus achieving what Bachelard considered the essential function of poetry.[15]

As the poems presented in this volume will confirm, Guillevic acknowledges no hierarchy. His direction has always been towards immanence. A blade of grass, a pebble on the roadside, a flower, a tree, a bird, the salt flats, a canal, the sea, including the loved one—the intermediary to it all—are equally important to his quest for the origin of origins.

Equating the act of poetic creation with the mystic experience of fusion with the whole is far from unique to Guillevic. He, however, increasingly lived it in his search for what lies behind any form of reality. This is probably best expressed in his own words from *Du pays de la pierre,* the last book of interviews which has just been posthumously published:

"Often in daily life, there is, all the same, a barrier between the human being, the poet and the world, and suddenly things change, there is an opening, a communion . . . I am in communion with the house in front of me, the tree . . .

. . . I write when the barrier breaks down. I am not the one who breaks it. It does that itself."[16]

Guillevic equates the poetic act with the gift of absolute love, the enactment of a passion for the world, (in the religious sense of the term).[17] This is why, to a certain extent, all Guillevic's poems could be considered love poems since his experience of love connects him with every form of being in the universe. His love poems, among the most powerful in all the world's repertoire of love poetry, sometimes explicitely adressed to the

---

[15] An unpublished letter of Bachelard to Guillevic attests to mutual recognition between the poet and the philosopher.

[16] Guillevic et Boris Lejeune, *Du pays de la pierre, Entretiens animés et présentés par Lucie Albertini,* Editions de la Différence, Paris, 2006, p.90, 91.

[17] Ibid, p.95.

loved one, sometimes indirectly alluding to the union with the self and the world achieved through love, evince the same search for the inner core of being. Hardly anyone, without relying on the crutches of religion, has better expressed the unifying power of love with cosmic knowledge, not the traditional romantic unity, but the all-encompassing and enlightening power that love bestows. It is not surprising, therefore, that his most stirring hommage to the loved one contains the luminous expression of a realisation which not only sums up a unique quality of relationship but epitomizes Guillevic's lifelong quest for the world's equation.

En toi	Within you
Le monde se résume	The world is summed up
Sans se réduire.	Not reduced.

"Magnificat," *Trouées*, 1981.

All these features of Guillevic's poems are well illustrated in the selection we present. There is a profound unity in Guillevic's work. All the themes found in this collection can be traced back to earlier poems: death, love, rocks, the sea, the now, the everyday, and beyond all objects of perception the founding necessity of silence. But, in contrast with the somewhat torn apart sensitivity of the earlier works there is a general agreement among readers and critics that, in the later works there is a deepening of focus, a greater mastery, a sense of fulfillment.

The poems selected for this collection come from six volumes written during the last twenty years of Guillevic's life, two of which were posthumously edited and introduced by Lucie Albertini Guillevic: *Quotidiennes* (2002) and *Present* (2004). From *Requis*, a five year (1977–82) meditation, gathering, in one sequential poem, 406 "quanta," as Guillevic used to name those lapidary glimpses of reality, we have selected the two poles of his inspiration: Thanatos and Eros. The first section offers an astonishingly clear-sighted experience of the moment of severance from the world. It includes a passage which seems, in retrospect, a poignant prediction:

Il reste à inventer	There still remains to invent
Le tombeau qui convient	A suitable grave
A ceux qui le refusent.	For those who refuse to have one.

Requis, p.10.

This wish has been heard and realized. At the request of the French Writer's Society, (Société des Gens de Lettres), the French National Board of Culture and Communication has given a unique authorization to inter Guillevic's ashes in the neolithic moors of his native land inside a Prehistoric National Historic Monuments Property. The site will be officialized on the occasion of the celebrations for the 100th anniversary of his birth. The "suitable grave" has indeed been invented for him.

Guillevic's great poem on the subject is not to be accounted for by the anticipation of the imminence of death in advanced age. His very first writings were haunted by death. *Le chant d'un mourant*, (The song of a dying man), published in a limited edition by Robert Blanchet in 2004, was written in 1930. *Requiem,* Guillevic's first publication in 1938, is a series of expressionistic verbal paintings, so to speak, of dead animals in the countryside. The young poet, however, was already overcoming dichotomies, for his dead animals are strikingly present. *Sphère* (1963), includes a poem entitled "De ma mort" (About my death) and there is also a particularly moving expression of his encounter with death in "Elegies" in which he evokes the death of his first adolescent love.

J'ai appris qu'une morte	I have learned that a dead girl,
Soustraite, évanouie,	Taken away, vanished,
Peut devenir soleil.	Can be the light of the sun.

Sphère, p.105.

If Guillevic's experience of love was attached to that of death, it simultaneously enhanced his urge to glorify life. Love poems are to be found in almost every volume of his work.

"Déjà" and "Magnificat" in *Trouées,* "Elle" in *Possibles Futurs* are known and appreciated throughout the world. The pages we have carved out of *Requis* epitomize his permanent hommage to love:

Mandataire Entre le nuage Et moi —	Mediator Between the cloud And me—
Dans les deux sens.	Both ways.

Requis p.116

With *Motifs* (1981–84) we are approaching the home ground of the poet, so to speak the original source of his call to poetry. We did not choose "The Sea" as the eponymous title of this volume because it happens to be the longest of all, but because for Guillevic, the sea is the primordial element, the mysterious connection with the unknown. This poem is a masterful counterpart to *Carnac* (1961). *Carnac,* a single book size poem, marks a true "renaissance" for Guillevic, a major coming into being of the full amplitude of his voice. In *Carnac,* the sea was standing at the edge of nothingness. There was still the sense of alterity between the observer and the observed, and even, at times, anxiety. Twenty years later, the sea asserts itself as Guillevic does then in his inner life:

Pourquoi pas moi La mer,	Why not me The sea,
Pourquoi pas moi Là-haut?	Why not me Up there?

I shall not comment in detail the poems included in this volume. It is a more appropriate task for Patricia Terry who entered their very fabric as she translated them and who selected most of them herself.

Within *Motifs,* I wish, however, to draw attention to the central notion of "Dehors-dedans"(Outside-inside), the outer versus the inner perception which lies at the core of all Guillevic's work. The title *Motifs* is ambivalent. It includes the juridicial sense of motivation or motive, and the project of painting outdoors introduced by the Impressionists with their decision to "*peindre sur le motif.*" Guillevic plays on both meanings of the word: his poems are inspired by the sites where he had his roots (motivation, motive), but they also have some pictorial quality although Guillevic's outscapes are always also inscapes.

There are indeed no verbal landscapes in *Motifs*, but the voicing of an inner perception of outer scapes, hence the fundamental significance of the notion of inner/outer perception which informs the entire volume of *Motifs*. Because Guillevic never describes, but penetrates from within what he observes, he achieves the contemporary painter's dream of making the invisible visible. This may greatly account for the widespread attraction Guillevic's poetry exerts on artists who undoubtedly find a real correspondence, in the Baudelairian sense of the term, between Guillevic and the artistic sensibility of his time.

By their titles alone, *Maintenant* (Now), *Quotidiennes* (Everyday) and *Present*, the three volumes from which we chose the following poems, emphasize Guillevic's commitment to capturing the immediacy of the instant, savouring every contour of its fleeting evanescence. They all focus on the poet's intensifying effort not to halt the passage of time, but not to allow any atom of the given present to escape. It is no surprise to discover in his interviews that Guillevic was a passionate reader of Proust. He undoubtedly shared with him the sense of the magic of things but also more particularly the recognition of the pervasive immanence of the past in the present. Proust was a contemporary of the first developments of quantum theory. Whether it was knowledge or intuitive synchrony with his time, he certainly perceived the limitations of the traditional space-time dichotomy. For Guillevic it was more than a concept, it was a life experience:

Ereintant	Exhausting
De se vivre	To live one's life
A trois dimensions,	In three dimensions
Alors que la quatrième	While the fourth
Crie dans le désert.	Cries aloud in the desert.

Requis, p.47.

Silence is at the very core of the entire work of Guillevic. We have therefore chosen to end the book with "*Du silence*" (Silence) in spite of our general preference for a chronological order. Written in spring 1994 and first published in 1995[18] before it was included in *Possibles Futurs* (1996), "Silence" stands out as a work of its own. It is the true epitome of Guillevic's poetic and spiritual itinerary. Guillevic frequently described himself as a "sculptor of silence."

"Poetry," says Guillevic again in *Vivre en poésie,* is like "the marriage of words and silence . . . a sculpture of silence."[19]

Moreover it is appropriate to end the book on the last words of Guillevic published in his lifetime:

Le silence, ma lumière	Silence, my light
Est devenue joie.	Has become joy.

---

[18] *Du Silence,* Guillevic, Ed. Pierre-Alain Pingoud, Pully, Switzerland, 1995. Although the title in English "silence" may seem to refer back more directly to "Le silence," in French, the addition of any "on," "about," "from," "or," or "of," which at first appears to be closer to the original "Du silence," would in fact suggest a treatise on silence instead of the intimate meditation on the poet's relation to silence which the poem explores. Hence the translator's choice for this volume.

[19] *Vivre en poésie,* p.186.

At the same time orphic and dionysiac, Guillevic knew and expressed more powerfully than many the joy of living through the sacrificial pain of writing:

Traversant la douleur Sacrificielle d'écrire:	Through the sacrificial Pain of writing:
Une joie.	A joy.

Inclus, p.126.

Moniquc Chefdor
Paris, January 2007.

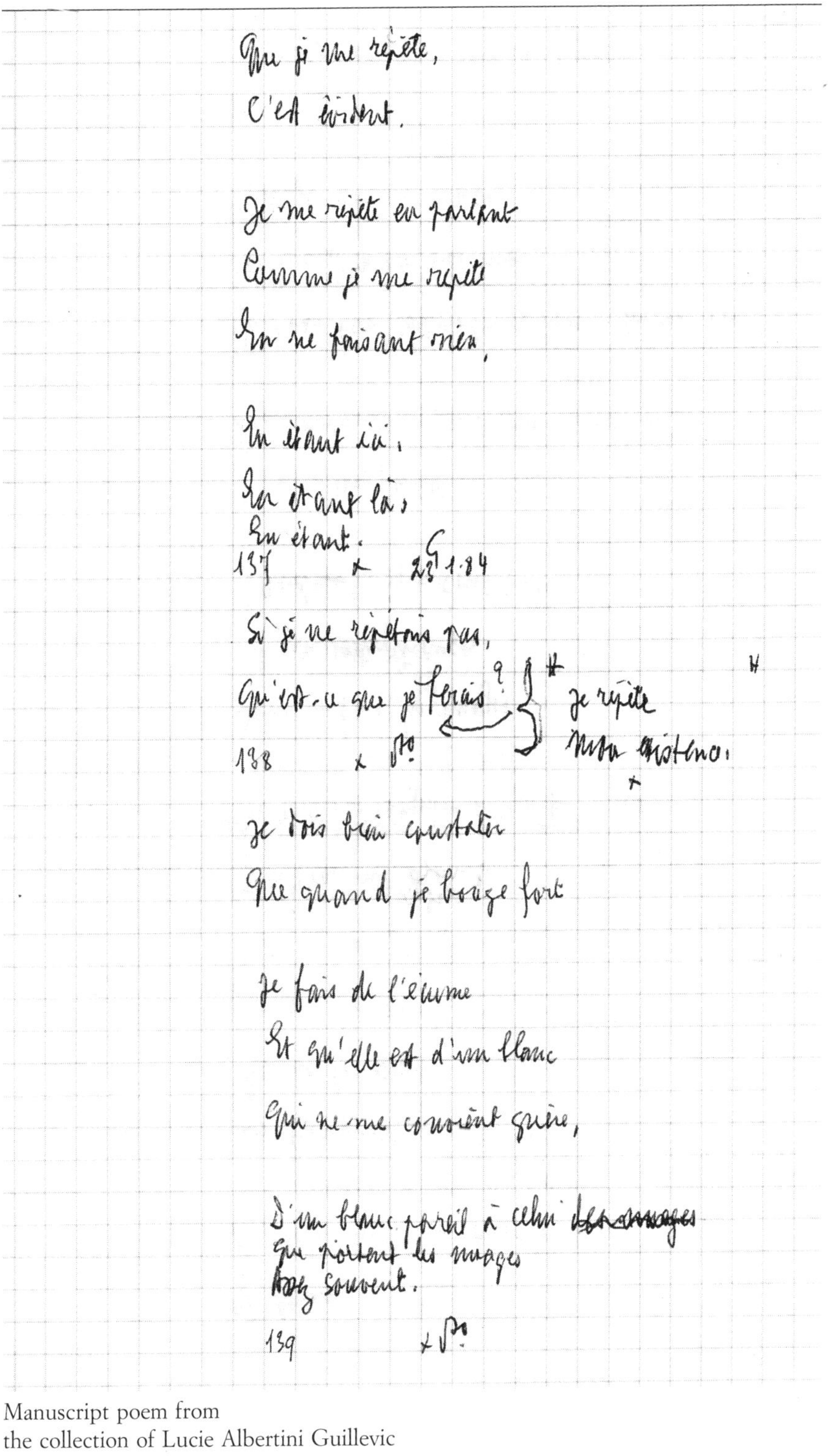

Que je me répète,
C'est évident.

Je me répète en parlant
Comme je me répète
En ne faisant rien,

En étant ici,
En étant là,
En étant.
137 × 23.1.84

Si je ne répétais pas,
Qu'est-ce que je ferais ? } je répète mon existence.
138 × St.

Je dois bien constater
Que quand je bouge fort

Je fais de l'écume
Et qu'elle est d'un blanc
Qui ne me convient guère,

D'un blanc pareil à celui ~~des nuages~~
Que portent les nuages
Assez souvent.
139 × St.

Manuscript poem from
the collection of Lucie Albertini Guillevic

6

Si c'est pour demander
Pourquoi le silence,

~~Il vaut mieux~~
~~que vous restiez~~
~~loin de l'autre.~~

Vous n'êtes pas d'ici.

24.4.73

Manuscript poem from
the collection of Lucie Albertini Guillevic

Translator's Preface

What has most of all attracted me to Guillevic is his ability to make us believe, actually experience, what we already know, those familiar realities of human life that tend to remain at a distance. Particularly impressive examples of this are found in the sequence of *Requis* in which death comes close enough to illuminate life, and *La Mer* in which the absolute indifference of the sea is more convincingly expressed than in any other work of art that I know. Guillevic projects no emotions into anything; the emotions come directly from what he perceives. We ourselves may have felt the indifference of the ocean, but this is still our own impression. Guillevic's words are from the ocean's point of view, and they carry a stunning conviction:

> For me
> Here's the difference
>
> Between someone drowned
> And a swimmer:
>
> The drowned
> Are no longer afraid.

The sea observes, with some surprise, how ignorant we are of the real state of affairs:

The funny thing
Is that some people
Plead with me.

Yet its sense of its own power gives rise to some questions; power in itself could be, in this case wants to be, innocent—the winds, after all, cause the storms. Or did something in the sea itself invite them?

I say
That I personally am not violent,

That my rages
Aren't really mine,

They belong to
The sun and the wind.

But it remains to be seen
If I'm not involved in it too,

It remains to be seen
If there isn't something in me
That may call out to them

On purpose.

But if that "something" exists, it can neither be identified nor influenced. More heart-felt is the realization that the very rocks will live and die, and the sea will remain in its absolute solitude.

Everywhere, Guillevic gives voice to the natural world, and that includes himself—the sea, the wind, rocks, flowers, but also the "Inside-Outside," that borderless region of the mind where perceptions have no true location. How can the tree we are looking at be said to be entirely outside us?

I see outside
What is within,

Within me
What is outside.

And the reader cannot be excluded from the poem, hence the many times when Guillevic uses "we," as in "We always want/ To go beyond" from *Maintenant.* More complex is the pronoun "you," which would seem to separate Guillevic and the reader, to address itself to an individual, one or the other. Paradoxically, as Guillevic uses it, "you" seems to make the unity of poet and reader more vivid. (Unfortunately for translation into English, the forms "toi" and "tu" denote an intimacy which "you" does not express.) This is especially true in the extraordinary sequence from *Requis* which evokes the last moments of life. That the imagined moment of death is primarily that of the poet becomes clear toward the end of the poem, when a specific loved one is mentioned. But earlier the "you" seems to be "us" rather than Guillevic; in either case the voice carries enormous authority. We feel that its instructions would apply to us as well, and the knowledge behind the words strikes us as real.

Gather up all
The will-power
You didn't use
In the course of your life.

Don't let it go
To waste.

Here again the poem advises that one pay attention to what is outside and what is inside, as they merge in the observing consciousness:

Best to try
Floating on your back

Looking at
Everything around you
And everything inside.

Whether the advice is being given to the poet or to the reader, whose voice is speaking? When we think of death, our own death, most of us shield ourselves from its reality. Death is far away, our belief in its inevitability remains abstract; even in moments of real danger it seems we will be spared. Guillevic, who wrote about death in his earliest books, gets beyond the barrier of the intellect, beyond his personal emotions, to visualize the last moments of life. This voice, which is objective, can express how last things—the smell of fresh-baked bread, a tree in bloom,—acquire the vividness, the absolute value they always had, the value of life itself.

Beyond perceptions, observations, emotions, and thoughts, is "silence," what Guillevic calls his kingdom, as described in the long poem called "Silence." The first page articulates the effort required to reach beyond the interior silence within the self toward

. . . the great
The total silence within my life

Where the world, I hope,
Will reveal to me something of itself.

To write a poem like "The Sea" requires an effort of concentration by which the poet identifies with an object in the world, putting himself in its place and speaking in its voice. The project of "Silence," is more courageous still. Even to name something keeps us separate from what we perceive. Guillevic narrates, in words, his journey into the wordless, the "kingdom" which has to be conquered over and over again because it requires the extinction of the self, which the self endlessly resists.

This kingdom is not an exclusion of the world; the silence of the self is not soundless. But the sounds that are heard, a bird's song, for example, are heard fully. The song comes from the bird, not from the poet, its songs are new to him, bring him ever more toward the center of the silence, make him want to sing himself, and he does sing. The poet's song will be words, but words that are, like the bird's song to which he responds, unexpected. They come from the natural world as it is without his intervention, in his absence.

Guillevic follows no guide other than his own instinct, acknowledges no spiritual tradition. Yet, as Monique Chefdor points out, his beliefs are compatible with those of Zen and Tibetan Buddhism, Hindu scripture. True knowledge and union with all things will come from a surrender of one's own experiences, personal emotions and preferences. Oriental meditation practices, different one from another, all express this fundamental effort to overcome the limitations of the self, its transience and lack of solidity, and find, in the non-self, wisdom, and, in wisdom, joy. Guillevic's "silence" is very much like what is called "Buddha nature."

An authentic poem will always surprise the poet, and then the reader. A translation must aspire to do the same, a project open to another kind of surprise. Translators, searching for "equivalence," hope that the reader of their work will have an experience comparable to that of a reader of the original. But that reader is the translator herself. "Salt Flats" was the first poem I selected for this collection. I had seen salt flats in France, but it didn't occur to me to identify with the water. In Guillevic's poem, the water, gradually disappearing, comes to understand its doom, watching the sky fade away, knowing that even the salt would leave. After reading the words of the salt flats, nothing could return them to the neutral, affectless state in which I had found them. That transformation was the experience I wanted to reproduce in English.

I have since discovered, however, that for Guillevic himself, the more important of the two elements was the salt. He compared it to the poems which are the product of the poet's life, what he leaves behind. Nothing in the translation had to be changed in response to this interpretation. One passage, however, hints at Guillevic's meaning. When the water, having "nothing more to offer / The boats/ Or the seagulls" says:

> And, bitter joke on us!
> We thought that meant
> We were useless.

The water, in my reading, was indeed useful, but only in the "ineluctable agony" of its disappearance. For Guillevic that death was the price of the salt, the substance of inestimable value which the water, unknowing, carried within it. Yet the salt is given no voice, and that of the water, in its poignancy, may remind us that art resists simple interpretations, and may suggest also that the translator's goal of equivalence might more prudently be expressed as transparency.

I would like to express my gratitude to Monique Chefdor for initiating this project and for the many valuable suggestions she has made. The translations owe much to her sensitive understanding of the texts. I am grateful also to Mme Lucie Albertini Guillevic for welcoming my work and for allowing our use of documents from her private archives.

My heartfelt thanks, as always, to Kathleen Micklow. It is a great comfort to pick up the phone and reach her, on the other side of the continent, when doubts strike or there seems no way through an impasse. Or simply to share a moment of particular admiration for the poet.

—Patricia Terry

from REQUIS (SUMMONED)
(1977–82)

Ne cherche pas . . .
(Gallimard, pp. 97–125)

Ne cherche pas
À savoir d'avance

Si,
Lors de ta fin,

Ce sera très haut,
Si ça descendra.

Sois
À ton niveau.

*

Ce ne sera pas
Franchir.

Ce sera
Flancher.

*

On essaiera
De faire la planche,

Regardant
Tout autour,

Tout dedans.

*

Don't try
To find out in advance

If,
At the end,

It will be very high up
Or come down.

Just stay
At your own level.

*

You won't be
Overcoming.

Only
Giving up.

*

Best to try
Floating on your back

Looking at
Everything around you

And everything
Inside.

*

Tu ne pourras plus
Tendre la main.

Rien non plus
Ne la saisira

Que la désertion.

*

On parle beaucoup,
À travers l'histoire,

De l'éponge posée
Sur certaines lèvres.

Pas dérisoires,
Toutes les dérisions.

*

Voir sourire un mort
N'est pas rareté.

Voir sourire
Un mourant.

*

You won't be able to
Hold out your hand.

There will be nothing
To grasp it

Except desertion.

*

There has been a lot of talk
Throughout history

About a sponge pressed against
Certain lips:

Some forms of derision
Are not derisory.

*

To see a smile on a dead person's face
Is not unusual.

To see a smile
On the face of a person dying.

*

Au dernier moment
Fleurit un cerisier

Qui vient s'offrir
Par la fenêtre.

*

Ce sera l'abandon
À la plongeante.

*

Que faire,
À cette heure-là,

De l'odeur
Du pain frais?

*

Pâle.

Une couleur
De transition.

*

At the last moment
A cherry tree blooms

And presents itself
At the window.

*

A deep dive
Into the loss of everything.

*

What can you do
At that moment

With the smell
Of fresh-baked bread?

*

Pale,

A color
Of transition.

*

Ne pas confondre
Avec la nuit.

Avec l'emphytéose
Des puits.

*

Suppose
Un long dernier moment.

Le sanglier blessé
Qui saigne contre toi.

*

Ne faites pas alors
De bruits de papier.

Trinquez
Si le coeur vous en dit.

*

Les paroles,
C'était pour avant.

Essaie maintenant
Un mot blêmi.

*

Don't confuse this
With night.

Or the long-term mortgage
Of a well.

*

Assume
A long last moment.

A wounded boar
Leaning against you, bleeding.

*

At that point don't make
Sounds like paper.

Offer a toast
If you feel like it.

*

Too late
For talk.

Now just try
A pallid word.

*

Pas de passage.
N'aie plus peur

Du tourbillon de vide
Qui aspire.

Pour l'heure,
C'est du sur-place.

*

Adieu, la rose—
Mais elle aussi.

Adieu,
La pierre.

Témoignera.

*

À de certains moments,
C'est tant de mains
Que tu voudras saisir

Pour les caresser toutes.

*

No way through.
Stop being afraid

Of the whirlwind of aspiring
Emptiness.

Now
You can only be where you are.

*

Farewell, rose
But, you too.

Farewell,
Stone.

Bear witness.

*

At certain moments
There are so many hands
You want to grasp

And caress them all.

*

Il t'en aura fallu
Des siècles

Pour peut-être accepter
L'inacceptable.

*

Épuise ton lot
À toi

Jusqu'au virage

Dans le plus jamais blanc
Ni coloré de rien.

*

Pour ce terminus,

Ramasse alors
Cette volonté

Qui au cours de ta vie
Ne t'aura pas servi.

Ne la laisse pas
Inemployée.

*

It will have taken you
Centuries

To accept, perhaps,
The unacceptable.

*

Use up your portion,
Yours

Until the turning

Into the never white again,
Nor colored by anything.

*

At this last stop,

Gather up all
The will-power

You didn't use
In the course of your life,

Don't let it go
To waste.

*

Plus besoin de boussole.

Plus besoin
D'adjectifs.

*

Il reste à inventer
Le tombeau qui convient
À ceux qui le refusent.

*

On ne sourira plus
À l'éternal soleil,

À l'enfant
Qui aime aussi
Les pissenlits.

*

No need for a compass any more,

No need for adjectives.

*

Remains to invent
A suitable grave
For those who refuse to have one.

*

Never again will you smile
At the eternal sun,

Or the child
Who shares your love
For dandelions.

*

Si, au dernier moment,

Tu peux encore
Penser,

J'aimerais
Que ce soit à elle

Et que le merle
Nous célèbre
Comme toujours.

*

Une étoile,
Tu sais bien,

Sera là
Au-dessus de toi,
Sur la gauche.

De ton mieux,
Tu la salueras.

*

Il n'y aura pas de nuage
Pour servir de carrosse.

*

If, at the last moment,

You can still
Think,

I would like you to think
Of her,

And may the blackbird
Sing as always
In our honor.

*

You know
There will be a star,

Right there,
Above you,
On the left.

Greet it
As best you can.

*

You won't have a cloud
For a carriage.

*

—Voir encore
De l'herbe

Et, au-dessus,
Le vent,

L'espace ouvert
À la lumière.

There will still be
The grass,

And wind
Above it,

Space opening
Into light.

Quelle est la capitale de l'absence? (Gallimard, pp. 115–125)

Quelle est
La capitale
De l'absence?

Sûrement pas elle,
Car elle

Est la capitale
Du corps,

Ici en attente.

*

Nuage,
Pas nuage.

Elle,
Pas nuage.

Elle,
Un corps.

Capital.

*

What is
The capital
Of absence?

She can’t be it,
For she

Is the capital
Of the body

Here waiting.

*

A cloud
Not a cloud

Herself,
Not a cloud.

Herself
A body.

Capital.

*

Mandataire

Entre le nuage
Et moi—
Dans les deux sens.

*

Qu'elle vienne le dire.

Celle du:
Être là,

Celle du:
Être là-bas

En même temps
Qu'ici.

*

Il y a des courants.

Aucun
Ne peut emporter

Son image fixée
Pour durer
Jusqu'au point final.

Le mouvement
Ici s'enracine.

*

Mediator

Between the cloud
and me—
Both ways.

*

Let her come and say it.

She who is
Being present,

She who is
Being there

At the same time
As here.

*

There are tides.

None
Can carry away

Her image held fast enough
To last
Until it all comes to an end.

Here movement itself
Takes root.

*

Besoin
De ses deux mains.

Besoin
De l'évidence.

*

Je jouerais du gong
À travers la nuit

Pleine de noir
Tremblant de bleu,

À travers les forêts
Mangeuses d'hectares.

Île contre île,
Je jouerais du gong,

Et l'océan
Viendrait me glisser:

Ne pleure pas.
Garde-la.

*

The need
For her two hands.

The need
For what can't be denied.

*

I would beat a gong
All through the nights

Full of blackness
Trembling with blue,

Through the land-devouring
Forests.

Island against island,
I would beat a gong,

And the ocean
Would come and whisper:

Don't cry.
Keep her.

*

Il y a des moments
Où elle est tellement là,

Contre toi,
En toi,
Ton absente,

Que tu sais
T'endormir heureux

Sous le bégaiement
Du corps voyageur
Qui t'enveloppe.

*

Elle,
Peut-être assise
Sur le pennage de la tranquillité,

Vient entière
Vers toi.

*

Elle aura bu
Toutes les nuances
De la rosée.

Ne te trouvera pas indigne
De prendre la suite.

*

At certain moments
She is so intensely there,

Close to you,
Within you,
Your absent one,

That you are able
To fall asleep happy

Under the stammering
Of that body so far away
Enveloping you.

*

She,
Who perhaps is seated
On the tranquility of molted feathers

Comes in her totality
Toward you.

*

She will have drunk
All thc nuances
Of the dew.

And will not think you unworthy
Of following her.

*

Essence

De toutes les essences
Devinées.

*

Quand elle vient,
Elle s'ouvre

Sans appoggiature.

*

Lisse.
Lisse.

Curieux
Qu'elle soit si lisse,

Taisant
Son ouverture.

*

Essence

Of all the essences
Imagined.

*

When she comes,
She opens

Without grace-notes.

*

Smooth.
Smooth.

Strange
That she should be so smooth.

Keeping silent
Her opening.

*

Derrière ce visage
Qu'elle porte

Et qu'elle jette vers l'extérieur,

Après
Cet apparent visage,

Un visage.

*

Où vas-tu,
Visage?

Que regardes-tu?
Qu'est-ce
Que tu attends?

Caresse
Ou quoi?

*

Behind the face
She is wearing

That she projects toward the outside,

After
That apparent face,

A face.

*

Where are you going,
Face?

What are you looking at?
What
Are you waiting for?

A caress,
Or something else?

*

Avant toute chose,
Visage

Je me mets à genoux
Devant toi,

Me tais comme l'escargot
Devant le soleil

Ou l'inverse.

*

Sur tes visages,

Le soleil couchant
Est percé
Par le soleil levant.

La nuit se mutile.

*

Visage autre
Encore
Sur visage

Encore et encore
Visage sur visage.

Et c'est sans fin?

*

First of all,
Face,

I kneel
In front of you,

As silent as a snail
Before the sun

Or the reverse.

*

On your faces,

The setting sun
Is pierced
By the rising sun.

Night is mutilated.

*

Still another
Face
Upon face

Again and again,
Face upon face.

And this will never end?

*

Le visage
Du plus profond
Des profondeurs?

Le visage en infraction
Avec les lois
Du terrestre?

Le visage donné
Par l'au-delà des sources?

*

Je l'ai trouvé

Comme on débouche
Une source.

J'y bois.
J'y plonge.

Je m'y songe
Immodérément.

*

L'obsurité
A peut-être envie,
Elle aussi,

D'être caressée.

*

The face
From the deepest
Of all depths?

The face
That violates
The terrestrial laws?

The face that was given
By what is beyond all springs?

*

I found it

The way you liberate
A spring.

I drink from it.
I dive into it.

I come into my own dream
Wildly.

*

Perhaps darkness
Also
Has the desire

To be caressed.

*

Sur nous,

Le fleuve-océan
Des années-lumière.

*

C'était
Au centre même
Du noyau.

*

Dans cet espace
Au-delà de l'espace,

Je n'appelle personne.

Over us,

The river-ocean,
The light-years.

*

It was
At the very center
Of the stone of a fruit.

*

In that space
Beyond space

I summon no one.

from MOTIFS (MOTIVES)
(1981–84)

LES MENHIRS

Il fallait qu'il y eût cette mer,
Cette baie où elle se repose,
Pense à elle-même,

S'interroge
Sur le mouvement,

Rame vers nous.

*

Nous sommes
De l'immobile en mouvement.

Nous traversons
La durée.

*

Nous sommes de la durée
Qui s'est arrêtée

Pour se voir passer.

*

THE MENHIRS

There had to be that sea,
And the bay where it rests,
Thinks about itself,

Wonders
About the movement,

Rows
In our direction.

*

We are
Immobility in motion.

We march
The length of time.

*

We are the passagc of time
Which has stopped

To see itself go by.

*

Nous sommes faits
Des cris des goélands

Arrivés au bout du monde,
Fatigués.

*

Nous avons été
Quelque chose d'important,

Nous avons gouverné.

*

Nous avons été
La musique
De ces landes sans fin.

*

Nous sommes
Une protestation
Contre l'espace vide.

Nous sommes le fruit
Du besoin d'avoir à toucher,
Du besoin de la verticale.

Nous sommes un cri
Contre le cri
Que nous incarnons.

*

We are made
Of the cries of seagulls

Who have reached the end of the world,
Exhausted.

*

We have been
Something important,

We have ruled.

*

We have been
The music
Of these endless moors.

*

We are
A protest
Against the empty space.

We are the fruit
Of the need to have something to touch,
The need for the vertical.

We are a cry
Against the cry
Whose incarnation we are.

*

Plantés là
Contre le balancement,

Contre la marée,
Contre le vent.

*

La mer—où est-elle?—
Vient à nous
Sous forme de pluie.

Pour nous battre?
Pour nous laver?

Rien
Que pour nous saluer?

Nourrir nos lichens?

*

Rooted here,
Opposed to swaying,

Opposed to the tide
Opposed to the wind.

*

The sea—where is it?
It comes to us
As rain.

To beat us?
To cleanse us?

Simply
To acknowledge us?

To nourish our lichens?

*

Lovés en nous,
Retirés en nous,

Voyant quand même
Et pas sans compassion,

Tout ce qui vient
Autour de nous
Et ne dure pas:

Ces nuages, ces herbes,
Ces gens.

*

Nous en avons vu
Se mettre à genoux

À la façon du soleil
Vers le soir

Comme si c'était nous
Qui les y incitions,

Comme si le couchant
Nous avait sacrés,

Afin que vers lui
Nous témoignions.

*

Coiled up inside ourselves
Withdrawn into ourselves,

But, even so, seeing,
And not without compassion

All that comes
Into our presence
And does not last:

Those clouds, grasses,
People.

*

We have seen some of them
Kneel down

The way the sun does
Toward evening

As if they did so
Because of us,

As if the sunset
Had made us holy,

Wanting us
To bear witness.

*

Ce n'est pas vers la justice
Que nous sommes
Une armée en marche.

C'est vers un équilibre difficile
Dans un demi-cercle
Avec une pierre plate

Où le sang peut couler.

*

Nous allons
Vers où l'on va
Quand on est arrivé.

We are an army
On the march,
And not toward justice,

But toward a precarious balance
In a semi-circle
Where there is a stone flat enough

For blood to flow.

*

We are on our way
Toward the destination
We have already reached.

LE CANAL

Je suis comparable
À ces moments
Où le temps ne passe pas –

Et qu'en faire?

*

Je suis un enfant mort-né
Du fleuve d'à côté.

Il vit ce que je rêve de vivre
Et que j'ai vécu.

*

Parfois je ressemble
À l'abcès
Qui veut éclater.

*

THE CANAL

I am comparable
To those moments
When time does not go by.

And what to do with it?

*

I am the stillborn child
Of the river close by

Which lives the life I dream of,
And that I have lived.

*

Sometimes I am like
An abcess
That wants to burst.

*

J'ai été cette eau
Différente
Qui remue,

Qui aspire
À la verticale.

*

J'ai été cette jument
Que je vois courir
Dans les prés.

*

Maintenant je ne suis

Que du poids
Qui s'est fait liquide

Et qui emploie son temps
À se peser.

*

Soumis, je porte
Barques, péniches,
Des choses qui glissent.

*

I have been that water,
So different,
In motion,

Aspiring
To the vertical.

*

I have been that mare
Galloping
In the meadows.

*

Now I am only

Weight
Which has become liquid

And all it does
Is weigh itself.

*

Docile, I carry
Boats, barges,
Things that glide.

*

Il n'y a que le vent
Pour venir me saluer.

Rares les oiseaux
Qui s'intéressent à moi.

*

Les poissons
Qui filent en moi
Ne m'ont pas choisi.

*

Mes écluses
Sont comme les distractions
Des gens sans passion.

*

Pour les feuilles mortes
Je suis bon.

Chez moi
On ne les ennuie pas.

*

Only the wind
Comes to greet me.

I don't attract
Many birds.

*

The quick fish
Inside me
Didn't choose to be there.

*

My locks
Might be entertaining
For passionless people

*

I am just good enough
For the dead leaves.

When they're with me
No one disturbs them.

*

Étant donné
Ce que je sens de mon poids,

Que doit peser
Tout ce qui m'entoure?

*

Bien.
Je ne suis pas riche,
Pas prometteur,

Mais j'ai le silence.

*

Je dis que je suis mort-né,

Mais la vie c'est aussi
Durer dans le silence,

Se ramasser
Autour de soi.

*

Considering what I can feel
Of my own weight,

What must be the weight
Of all my surroundings?

*

Granted.
I am not rich,
Not promising,

But I have silence.

*

I say that I am stillborn,

But life is also
A holding on in silence,

Holding oneself
Close.

*

Je finirai quand même

Par arriver
À l'empire des mouettes

Et je me retrouverai
Eau en mouvement.

*

Je ne me saisis pas
Dans tout mon volume

Et pourtant mon volume
Est présent

Dans chacun de mes points.

*

En moi l'eau
Jamais ne se brise,
Sauf dans les écluses,

Mais les écluses
Ce n'est pas moi.

*

In the end, one day

I'll reach
The empire of seagulls

And find myself again
Water in motion.

*

I don't have a grasp
On my whole volume

And yet my volume
Is present

Wherever I am.

*

The water never breaks
Within me,
Except inside the locks,

But the locks
Are not me.

*

Je suis encadré,
Très encadré,
C'est vrai,

Est-ce que cela
Empêche mon amitié
Avec les nuages, l'azur?

*

On n'accourt pas tellement
Se noyer chez moi.

On préfère les fleuves,
Leurs remous.

*

Par définition
Je ne suis pas naturel,

Venez fouiller dans mes intérieurs
Et vous toucherez
De la nature.

*

J'ai en moi
Comme un écheveau de bien-être
Que je dévide lentement.

*

I am enclosed,
Tightly enclosed,
That's true,

Does that prevent
My friendship
With the clouds, the blue sky?

*

Not many come running here
To drown themselves.

They prefer the rivers,
Their currents.

*

By definition,
I am not natural.

Come and explore inside me
And you will touch
Nature.

*

I possess
Something like a skein of well-being
That slowly I unwind.

*

Mon immobilité
Rassure.

Même moi.

*

Quand le soleil arrive
Quelque chose
Change dans mon ventre.

*

Je ne me vois pas
Mais j'imagine

Que pour qui me regarde longtemps
Je ressemble à l'œil du chat.

*

Comment me reposer
De mon repos?

Je me tricote.

My immobility
Is reassuring,

Even for me.

*

When the sunlight reaches me,
Something
Changes inside my belly.

*

I don't see myself,
But I imagine

If you looked at me for a long time
I'd resemble a cat's eye.

*

How do I rest
From my resting?

Knitting myself.

LE DEHORS-DEDANS

Je suis dedans.
Je suis dehors.

Dans le dehors-dedans.
Dans le dedans-dehors.

*

Pierre qui roule
N'amasse pas mousse.

Sauf en moi.

*

L'aile du pigeon
Bat en moi.

En moi, le pigeon
Se pose sur une branche,

L'abeille
Butine un coquelicot.

*

THE OUTSIDE-INSIDE

I am inside.
I am outside.

In the outside-inside.
In the inside-outside.

*

The rolling stone
Gathers no moss,

Except within me.

*

The pigeon's wing
Beats inside me.

Inside me the pigeon
Perches on a branch,

The bee
Plunders a poppy.

*

Je vois hors de moi
Ce qui est en moi,

En moi
Ce qui est hors de moi.

*

L'océan
Roule mes vagues

Et m'ignore.

*

Je me lève
Pour le voir en moi.

Je m'assieds
Pour avec lui m'entretenir.

*

Le coq
Me chante mon réveil.

*

I see outside
What is within,

Within me
What is outside.

*

The ocean rolls
My waves,

Paying no attention to me.

*

I stand up
To see it within me.

I sit down
To have a conversation with it.

*

To me the rooster
Sings my awakening.

*

Entre moi
Et ce que je regarde

L'espace
N'est pas l'espace,
Mais un réseau.

*

Je me place mal
Dans ce qui cuit,
Dans ce qui gèle.

Il me faut
Une température
À ma mesure.

*

Je ne vis pas
Dans ce qui va très vite.

Je vis plus aisément
Dans le rocher
Que dans la flèche.

*

Between me
And what I am looking at

Space
Is not space,
It's a network.

*

I find uncongenial
Anything being cooked,
Or anything freezing.

I need
A temperature
More like my own.

*

I can't live
In anything moving too fast.

I live more easily
In a rock
Than in a steeple.

*

Je n'entre pas
Dans le tonitruant.

Je reste longtemps
Dans ce qui paraît dormir.

*

On ne m'expulse pas.
Je choisis parfois le départ.

Si c'est partir.

*

Viens, la lune,
Viens

Mettre fin
À ces rapports
Qui n'en sont pas.

*

Cacophony
Does not attract me.

I linger
Where something seems to be asleep.

*

I can't be forced to leave.
Sometimes I choose to.

If leaving is what that is.

*

Come here, moon,
Come here

And make an end
To these apparent
Relationships.

*

Comme si l'on pouvait
Y mettre fin,

Avec toi,
Lune du dehors
Et du dedans,

Royaume conquérant.

*

Je ne traverse pas
Le mur.

Le mur
Me perce.

*

Pas de brasier.

L'approche de l'âtre,
L'ombre tiède.

*

On est là
Où l'on est bien,

Avec ce que l'on a
Dans le dehors-dedans de soi.

*

As if they could be
Ended,

Between you,
Moon outside
And you, moon inside,

Conquering kingdom.

*

I don't go through
The wall,

The wall
Goes through me.

*

No raging flames.

Just close enough to the hearth,
The warm shadows.

*

There
I feel at ease

With what I have
In the inside-outside of my self.

*

Le tout est de savoir
Qu'on peut s'apprivoiser
Le dehors-dedans.

*

La groseille:
Le comble
Du dehors-dedans.

Je vis bien
La groseille.

*

Il n'y a que moi
Que je vois mal
Du dehors.

Même dans la glace.

C'est pour ça sans doute
Que je vois mal
Mon dedans.

*

Everything depends
On knowing that you can tame
That inside-outside.

*

The gooseberry:
Perfect image
Of the inside-outside.

I really saw
The gooseberry.

*

The only thing
I can't see from the outside
Is myself.

Even in a mirror.

No doubt that's the reason
I find it hard to see
My inside.

*

La fourmi
Rejoint à travers moi
La fourmilière

Que je n'ai pas envie
D'avoir en moi.

*

Curieux
Qu'en moi les choses

Perdent beaucoup
De leurs couleurs.

*

Je reçois les racines
Du tilleul.

Je les conforte
Dans la douceur.

*

Je ne filtre pas
La rivière.

*

The ant
Goes through me to return
To the ant hill

That I really don't want
To have inside me.

*

Strange
That things inside me

Tend to lose
Their colors.

*

The linden tree
Offers me its roots.

I comfort them
Gently.

*

I'm not a filter
For the river.

*

Je me fais,

Ne me défais pas
Avec le nuage.

*

Je suis
La nappe phréatique
De toutes les sources.

*

Pas de vitre à briser
Entre le dehors et moi.

*

En moi
De l'immense

Pour contenir tout ça.

*

L'espace
Est ce qui stagne

En dehors
De mon dehors.

I take shape,

Don't dissolve me
With clouds.

*

I am
The water table
Of all springs.

*

No pane of glass to break
Between the outside and me.

*

Immensity
Within me

To contain all that.

*

Space
Is what stagnates

Outside
Of my inside.

LES SALINES

Nous sommes très plates,
Trop fragmentées pour que le vent
Nous fasse plus qu'un friselis.

Nous ne voyons rien
Que ce qui passe
Au-dessus de nous,

Surtout
Les nuages, les goélands, les mouettes,
Quelques insectes.

*

De la même substance que la mer
Nous ne sommes plus la mer,

Son étendue, sa passion,
Son avidité.

Pour nous le calme,
La méditation
Vers la disparition.

*

SALT FLATS

We lie very close to the ground,
So fragmented the wind can do no more
Than ruffle our surfaces, slightly.

We see nothing
Except what passes
Above us,

Mostly
Clouds, terns, seagulls,
A few insects.

*

In substance the same as the sea,
We are the sea no longer,

Its far reach, its passion,
Its greed.

On our side there is calm,
Meditation
On the way to disappearance.

*

Nous savons que bientôt
Nous ne serons plus de l'eau,

Qu'il ne restera de nous
Que de la vapeur absente
Et des tas de sel assez blancs

Que nous bercions
Sans nous en douter.

*

Quand nous avons été
Séparées de la mer,

Nous n'avons pas compris
Ce qu'on voulait de nous.

*

En nous notre mort
N'était pas écrite.

Nous étions encore
Tellement pareilles

À ce que nous quittions
En entrant dans l'étier.

*

We know that soon
We won't be water any more,

All that remains of us
Will be an absent mist
And salt piles, more or less white.

We never realized
We were rocking them within us.

*

When we were cut off
From the sea,

We didn't understand
What was expected of us.

*

Nowhere was our death
Inscribed.

We were still
So very much the same

As what we were leaving
When we entered the canal.

*

Après, cela fut lent.

C'est peu à peu
Qu'il nous a fallu voir

Que nous devenions
Cette pellicule
Qui s'épaississait
En s'amenuisant.

*

Nous n'avons plus
Intéressé les barques,
Ni les mouettes.

Totale maintenant
Notre solitude,

Et, dérision,
Nous l'avons prise
Pour l'inutilité.

*

Then, it took a long time.

It was little by little
That we were forced to understand

We were becoming
That film
Growing thicker
As it diminished.

*

We had nothing more to offer
The boats
Or the seagulls.

Total now
Our solitude.

And, bitter joke on us!
We thought that meant
We were useless.

*

Nous le savons
À travers des voisines:

Bientôt on marchera
Là où nous sommes étalées.

On y ratissera le sel,
On y fera des tas
Plus hauts que nos désirs.

*

Il reste donc à vivre
Cette agonie déterminée.

Il y en a qui savent
Quand ce sera la fin,

Exactement.

*

Nous aurons eu le temps
D'approfondir le ciel,

Mieux que quand nous étions
La vague et ses dessous.

Nous aurons tout le temps
De le voir s'effacer

*

This we've learned
From the neighbors:

Soon, people will be walking
Where we are spread out.

They will rake the salt,
Make it into piles
Higher than our desires.

*

It remains for us to live out
That ineluctable agony.

There are some who know
When it will come to an end,

Exactly.

*

We will have had time
To make a real study of the sky

More thorough than when we were
Waves and the depths below them.

We will have time enough
To watch it fade away

*

Même le sel s'en ira,

Ne se souviendra pas
De nous, de nos folies
Dans les tempêtes

Et autrement.

*

L'air n'a jamais été plus doux,
Plus fait pour nous.

Even the salt will leave,

Won't remember
Our extravagance
In storms

And otherwise.

*

The air has never been softer,
More to our liking.

The salt flats as Guillevic knew them. They no longer exist.

photo courtesy of Monique Chefdor

LA MER

Pourquoi pas moi,
La mer,

Pourquoi pas moi
Là-haut?

*

Est-ce que je suis faite
Pour le goémon?

Est-ce qu'il est fait
Lui, pour moi?

*

Sûr
Que je rumine.

Qu'est-ce que j'ai d'autre
À faire?

*

THE SEA

What about me,
The sea,

Why couldn't I
Be up there?

*

Am I made
For the kelp?

Or the kelp made
For me?

*

Of course
I mull things over.

What else do I have
To do?

*

Se jeter dans la mer,
Disent les gens.

Mais moi, dans quoi
Puis-je me jeter?

*

Le soleil
Est un œil
Sur moi,

Et moi je n'ai
Que ma surface

Et mes essais
De mouvement.

*

On parle de moi

Et moi
Je ne sais parler
Que de moi, la mer.

*

Appelez-moi océan
Pour que ça me change.

*

People talk about
Throwing themselves into the sea.

But what do I have
To throw myself into?

*

The sun
Is an eye
Upon me.

And all I have
Is my surface

And my attempts
At movement.

*

People talk about me.

But I can only talk about
Myself,
The sea.

*

Call me ocean –
That would give me a change.

*

Pour vous,
Je ne suis qu'une voix,

Mais vous n'entendez
Que celle que j'ai
Pour le dehors.

*

On me caricature
Avec la vache de brume.

C'est tout
Ce qu'ils ont trouvé
Pour m'imiter.

*

C'est indiscutable:
Je suis la mer.

Il faut quelquefois
Me le rappeler.

*

Qui se rassemble s'assemble,
Dit-on.

Mais moi
Avec quoi?
Avec qui?

*

For you
All I am is a voice,

But you only hear
The one I have
For outside.

*

They imitate me
with the fog horn,

A caricature,
The best
They can do.

*

No question about it:
I'm the sea.

Sometimes I have to
Remind myself.

*

Birds of a feather flock together,
They say.

But me?
With what?
With whom?

*

Ce besoin
De se répéter,
Vague après vague.

*

Après tout,
Les ailes du goéland
Ce sont les miennes.

*

Cette eau
Qui s'en va en vapeur
Qui me revient en pluie,

Ne m'apporte
Souvenir de rien.

*

J'ouvre le regard des hommes
Sur l'infini.

Mais moi, c'est leur regard sur moi
Qui m'y jette.

*

This need
To repeat myself
Wave after wave.

*

After all,
The wings of the seagull
Are mine.

*

That water
Which leaves me as mist
And returns as rain

Doesn't bring me memories
Of anything.

*

I open the eyes of humans
To the infinite.

But I'm thrown into it
By the way they look at me.

*

Je suis obligée
De me laisser colorer
Par le ciel inconstant.

*

Ce n'est pas
Que j'aie tellement peur.
Depuis tout ce temps!

*

La crevette
En sait peut-être davantage
Sur moi.

*

Bien sûr
Que je ne suis pas indifférente
À l'égard de mes baleines,

Pas plus à mes algues,
À mon plancton,
À mes palourdes.

Nous tenons ensemble.

*

No way
Not to take on the colors
Of the inconstant sky.

*

Not that it
Frightens me so much
After all this time!

*

Most likely the shrimp
Are better informed
About me.

*

I am certainly not
Indifferent
To my whales,

Nor to my seaweeds,
My plankton,
Or my clams.

We're in this together.

*

Les horizontales,
Ça me connaît,

Mais, en fait, ce ne sont jamais
Que des portions de la sphère terrestre.

*

Le vent essaie bien
De me bercer,

Mais il n'en résulte
Que quelques rides
À la surface.

*

Les rochers
M'aident parfois

À sentir ma fraîcheur.

*

As for horizontals,
My all too familiars,

They're never more than segments
Of the terrestrial sphere.

*

The wind does try
To rock me,

Achieving only
A few wrinkles
On the surface.

*

Sometimes the rocks
Help me

To feel how cool I am.

*

En moi,
Ça grouille beaucoup,
Certes,

Mais c'est peu de chose.

Ce qui m'est le plus présent
C'est mon volume,
C'est ma pesanteur.

*

Pourquoi les arbres
Peuvent-ils demeurer
À la verticale—

Et moi non?

*

Malgré tout
Ce qu'on croit voir
De moi, sur moi, en moi,

L'immobilité
Est mon principe.

*

Inside me
There's a lot of churning around,
Sure.

But that's trivial.

What I'm most aware of
Is my volume,
My weight.

*

Why is it that trees
Can stand there,
Vertical –

And I can't?

*

In spite of everything
People think they understand
Of me, about me, in me,

Immobility
Is what I consider fundamental.

*

Quand ma surface
Est fatiguée de la lumière,

Elle se laisse couler
Dans ma profondeur.

*

Exilée en moi-même—
Et quel pouvoir?

*

Si j'essayais
De roucouler?

Si j'essayais
De remonter les fleuves?

Si j'essayais
De nager dans l'air?

*

Je veux considérer
Que le soleil levant
Est mon fruit.

*

When my surface
Gets tired of the light,

It lets itself drop down
Into my depths.

*

Exiled within myself
And what powers?

*

If I tried
To coo?

If I tried
To go up the rivers?

If I tried
To swim in the air?

*

I want to think
That the rising sun
Is my fruit.

*

Lorsque je ne suis pas bien
C'est que je ne suis pas
Dans ce qui est mon avenir.

*

Pas étonnant
Que ce soit en moi

Que naissent les crabes
Avec leurs pinces
À couper les doigts.

*

Si le vent
Était plus puissant.

Si la lune
Était plus puissante.

*

When all is not well with me
It's because I'm not in the present
Of my future.

*

No surprise
That I am the birthplace

Of crabs
With their claws
Made to cut fingers.

*

If the wind
Were more powerful.

If the moon
Were more powerful.

*

J'ai envie parfois
Que tout remue,
Se bouscule en moi
Depuis les profondeurs.

J'ai envie parfois
Que tout se fige en moi
Jusqu'aux vagues
De la surface.

*

Pourquoi
N'entrerais-je pas
En dissidence
Avec moi-même?

*

J'ai longuement bercé
Un rameau de je ne sais quel arbre
Et nous avions l'air

D'être de connivence, un peu
De la même famille.

*

Sometimes I want
My very depths
To be in motion
With everything colliding.

Sometimes I want
Everything to come
To a stop, including the waves
On the surface.

*

Why
Shouldn't I
Differ
With myself?

*

For a long time I cradled
A branch from some nameless tree
And we seemed

To be accomplices, almost
Part of the same family.

*

Où suis-je
Le plus moi-même,

Dans ma partie
Profonde et noire

Ou dans ma partie
Plus ou moins mobile
Et plus ou moins claire?

*

J'aime beaucoup moins
Toucher du fer que du bois.

Qu'il coule
Jusqu'au fond de moi,
Jusqu'à la terre.

C'est tout
Ce que je peux pour lui.

*

Where am I
The most myself,

In my darkest
Depths

Or where I am
More or less mobile
With more or less brightness?

*

I don't like the feel
Of metal. I prefer wood.

Let metal sink
Down to my depths,
Down to the ground.

That's all
I can do for it.

*

On pourrait croire
Que je me fatigue
De faire une vague après l'autre
Encore et encore.

Mais non!
Parce que je ne suis jamais sûre
De réussir
Celle que je commence.

*

Poulpe,
Ne sois pas si fier.

J'ai fait
Beaucoup mieux
Que toi.

*

You might think
I'd get tired
Of creating waves, over and over again
And then still more.

Not at all!
Because I'm never sure
I'll succeed
With the one I'm just beginning.

*

Octopus,
Don't be so proud.

You're far
From the best
I've done.

*

Je vois bien,
Quand les gens me regardent,

Qu'ils se demandent
Ce que je signifie,

Comme si chaque chose
Devait signifier

Et plus
Que pour soi-même.

*

Vous qui ne voyez de moi
Que ma surface,

Pensez que j'ai cette profondeur
Qui me rassure
Et parfois m'exalte.

*

Oui, je suis ivre,
Tout à fait ivre

De lucidité.

*

I can see
When people look at me

That they are wondering
What I mean,

As if everything
Had to have meaning

And not just
For itself.

*

You who see nothing of me
But my surface,

Think of the depths which are mine.
They give me reassurance
And sometimes exaltation.

*

Yes, I am drunk,
Completely drunk,

On lucidity.

*

Parmi tous ceux qui me regardent
Il y en a

Qui me demandent
Ce qu'ils sont,

Me le demandent
À moi, la mer.

Pourquoi n'est-ce pas au ciel,
Que moi-même j'interroge,

Allez savoir sur quoi.

*

Les nuages,
Bien, les nuages.

Ils viennent de moi,
Font semblant
De l'ignorer,

Mais je les récupérerai.

*

Among all of those who look at me
There are some

Who ask me
What they are.

Ask that
Of me, the sea.

Why don't they question the sky
As I do,

Guess about what!

*

Clouds
Well, as for clouds

They come from me;
They pretend
Not to know that.

But I'll get them back.

*

Si je devais
Croire en un dieu,

La lumière
Serait mon Dieu.

*

Valsez, poussières,
Devant moi
Sur les terres.

Si vous venez ici,
Je vous absorberai,

Ni vu, ni connu.

*

Je vois, moi aussi,
Et je sais

Ce que c'est qu'une mouette
Me frôlant au soleil levant.

*

If I were to believe
In a god,

Light
Would be my God.

*

You, dust,
Waltzing
Over the land.

If you come my way,
I'll absorb you,

Out of sight, out of mind.

*

I am not blind,
And I know

What a seagull is,
Skimming my surface at sunrise.

*

Je sais ce que c'est
Qu'un tremblement.

Mais qu'y a-t-il
De moins ordonné

Que le tremblement sur moi
De la lumière avant midi?

*

Enfouissons-nous,
Enfouissons-nous.

Oublions
La surface.

*

Je fais du mal
Lorsque j'avale?

Qu'est-ce que j'y peux?

*

Je suis toujours
Comme en train de bouillir—

Et je n'ai rien à cuire.

*

I know all about
Tremors

But is there anything
More random

Than the trembling of the light
Passing over me just before noon?

*

Let's go down into the depths,
Into the depths.

Forget
The surface.

*

I do harm
When I swallow?

What can I do about that?

*

It's as if I were
Always boiling

Without anything to cook.

*

Je ne ferai
Jamais d'ombre durable

Et ça me manque.

*

J'ai vu des roses
Auprès de moi, dans des jardins,

S'épanouir
Pour être à l'horizontale
Comme je suis.

*

Je me tends,
Oui, je me tends

Et je ne sais pas vers quoi.

*

Le sable est peut-être
Fatigué de moi
Et je le comprends.

Mais moi, jamais
Je ne me fatigue
De rien.

*

I'll never create
A lasting shadow

I wish I could.

*

I have seen roses
In gardens close by

Arch their petals far enough back
To be as horizontal
As I am.

*

I reach out
Yes, I reach out

And I don't know toward what.

*

The sand may be
Tired of me,
And I understand that.

But I
Am never tired
Of anything.

*

Je suis une page blanche

Sur quoi rien ne s'écrit
Que ma présence.

*

Je n'ai rien fait
Pour être là—

Et si je devais m'en plaindre,
Je ne saurais à qui, à quoi.

*

Qu'est-ce qui pour moi
Différencie

La coccinelle
Du clocher?

*

Je me reposerai,
Je me reposerai

Quand je l'aurai voulu,
Lorsque le temps

Me manquera
Pour la curiosité.

*

I am a blank page

On which nothing is written
But my presence.

*

It isn't my fault
That I am here—

And if I wanted to complain,
I wouldn't know to whom, to what.

*

From my point of view
What's the difference

Between a ladybug
And a steeple?

*

I will rest,
I will rest,

When I want to,
When I won't have enough

Time
For curiosity.

*

Les étoiles me supplient
De les changer de place

Et moi je les trouve bien
Là où elles sont.

*

Un poète a parlé
D'uraltes Wehen vom Meer,

Du souffle de la mer
Plus vieux que le temps.

Il se trompait.
Je suis toujours

En train
De m'accoucher.

*

Ils ont fait des phares
Pour signaler que vient la terre,

Comme si le mélange de nos souffles
Ne suffisait pas.

*

The stars beg me
To change their places,

But, personally, I like them
Just as they are.

*

A poet spoke about
Uraltes Wehen vom Meer,

The breathing of the sea,
Older than time.

He was wrong.
I am always

In the process
Of giving birth to myself.

*

They made lighthouses
To show that land was close,

As if the mingling of our breath
Wasn't enough.

*

En moi aussi
Ça pousse.

En moi aussi
Je sens des verticales
Se dessiner.

*

Je connais peu
Ce plus profond en moi
Qui me donne à moi-même.

C'est ma faiblesse
Que de trop me complaire

Au spectacle de tout
Ce qui n'est pas en moi

Et me distrait de moi.

*

Even in me
That stuff grows.

Even in me
I feel verticals
Forming.

*

I'm not much acquainted
With what is deepest in me,
And gives me to myself.

It's my weakness
To take too much pleasure

In the spectacle of all
That's outside me

And distracts me.

*

Mes limites
C'est la pesanteur
Qui me les assigne

Entre ce fond en moi
Et cet air au-dessus
Où je vais me cogner.

Sur mes côtés
J'ai quelque latitude
Et j'en profite.

*

Pour m'assécher,

Il en faudrait beaucoup
Des comme toi,

Soleil.

*

Si ces sempiternelles marées
M'amusent ou pas,

Demandez-le à ces brinquebalements,
Demandez-le aux plages.

*

My limits
Are set
By gravity

Between my depths
And that air above
Where I hit my head.

On my sides
I have some latitude,
And I use it to my advantage.

*

To get me dry

Would take good many
Like you,

Sun.

*

To find out if those ever-recurring tides
Amuse me or not,

Ask all that rocking and rolling about,
Ask the beaches.

*

Quelque chose d'assez pareil

Régit le grain du granit
Et cette addition de gouttes
Que je suis aussi.

*

Je n'ai jamais
Demandé à quoi que ce soit
D'avoir pitié de moi.

*

Il arrive que la nuit
Je suis seule
À me distinguer du reste.

*

Longues les heures
Où je n'ai affaire
Qu'à moi-même—

Et ce ne sont pas
Les pires.

*

Something rather similar

Determines the grain of granite
And that accumulation of drops
Which makes me too.

*

I've never asked
Anything at all
To take pity on me.

*

Sometimes at night
I am the only one who can tell
Where I end and the rest begins.

*

The hours are long
When I only deal
With myself—

And those aren't
The worst.

*

Je ne sais rien
De toutes ces ondes
Que me traversent.

Je n'écoute que moi.

*

Ce n'est pas
Parce que meurt le jour
Que je vis mon agonie.

*

Aller plus loin, oui,
Mais à travers quoi?

*

Quelle tête ils feraient
Si je me retournais

Et s'ils me voyaient à l'envers
Sens dessus dessous?

*

I know nothing about
Those vibrations of sound
That pass through me.

I only listen to myself.

*

It is not
Because the day dies
That I live my death-throes.

*

To go further, yes,
But across what?

*

Imagine the expression on their faces
If I turned over

And they saw me
Upside down!

*

Je m'enfonce
Dans des anfractuosités,

Je me roule sur des plages,
Je coule dans des bateaux,

Et je ne saurais dire
Ce que c'est que couler.

*

Parfois, dans les tempêtes,
On dirait

Que c'est à moi-même
Que je m'en prends.

*

Le plus drôle
C'est qu'il y a des gens
Qui m'implorent.

*

Saccades, saccades,

Pourquoi n'aurais-je pas droit
Moi aussi
À des saccades?

*

I hurl myself
Into the crevices of rocks,

I roll over beaches,
I go down into boats,

And I really couldn't tell you
How it feels to go down.

*

Sometimes, in storms,
It seems

That I'm furious
With myself.

*

The funny thing
Is that some people
Plead with me.

*

Jolted, jolted,

Why shouldn't I
Be jolted
Too?

*

Qu'est-ce qu'on ne se raconte pas
Quand on a pour soi
Tant de temps?

*

Si j'aimerais être frôlée?
J'aimerais l'être plus
Entre les continents.

*

Si ça ne dépendait que de moi,
Je serais gentille
Probablement,

Mais allez donc en parler
Au vent, à l'orage.

*

Certes, je fais du noir
Dans mes profondeurs,

Mais je n'ai pas le droit
Comme les rochers
De fabriquer de l'ombre.

*

No end to self-delusion
When one has
So much time.

*

Would I like to have something brush against me?
I wish there were more of that
Between the continents.

*

If it were all up to me,
I'd be nice,
Probably,

But talk about that
With the wind, with the thunder.

*

It's true that I create darkness
In my depths.

But unlike the rocks
I have no right
To make shadows.

*

Ils ont beau dire,

Pour soi-même
On n'est pas immense—

Et l'infini
N'est que dans les nombres.

*

Ceux
Qui nagent en moi,

Croient sans doute,
S'ils croient quelque chose,
Que pour moi ils existent.

*

Quoi désirer
De plus fort que moi?

*

C'est vrai
Ce que dit ce nuage,

Qu'à moi non plus
Il ne m'est pas donné de m'asseoir.

*

Regardless of what they say,

No one is immense
For himself—

And the infinite
Is only a matter of numbers.

*

Those
Who swim in me

No doubt believe,
If they believe anything,
That I am aware of their existence.

*

What is there to desire
More powerful than I am?

*

What this cloud says
Is true,

Neither of us
Gets to sit down.

*

Je ne fais pas exprès
D'user les rochers.

*

Je n'use d'ailleurs
Que ce qui en moi
Ne bouge pas.

Je n'use
Ni les requins,
Ni les goémons—

Et je supporte l'usure
Des reflets des nuages.

*

Je n'use pas les noyés.

Qu'à leur gré
Ils se défassent.

*

Je ne donnerais pas
Un de mes crabes,
Une de mes crevettes,

Pour être un jour
Autre chose.

*

I don't wear away the rocks
On purpose.

*

In fact, the only things in me
That I wear away
Don't move.

I don't wear away
The sharks
Or the kelp—

And I withstand being worn away
By the reflections of clouds.

*

I don't wear away the drowned.

Let them fall apart
If they want to.

*

I wouldn't give
One of my crabs,
One of my shrimp,

To get to be
Something else.

*

Moi je n'ai pas de contact
Avec ce soleil

Qui rougit avant
De disparaître
Derrière moi.

*

L'air, oui,
L'air me connaît.

Nous avons dû
Être quelque part ensemble
Dans une matrice,

La grande.

*

I myself have no contact
With the sun

Which turns red before
Disappearing
Behind me.

*

The air, yes,
The air knows me.

We must have been
Together somewhere
In a womb,

The big one.

*

En ce temps-là
Il y avait

Ce que l'oubli
Ne peut effacer.

Reste que l'on aime
Ce qui n'est pas,
Ce qui n'est plus,

Ce qui doit devenir,
Qui doit rester

Ce qui de nous
N'est pas de nous,

Mais notre nous
Plus nous-mêmes que nous.

*

Tout ce qu'on peut dire
De moi, que je dis
Moi-même

Dont je suis
Le motif en apparence.

*

At that time
There was

What even forgotten
Is not erased.

And so we love
What doesn't exist,
What doesn't exist any more,

What is to come
What is to remain

What in us
Doesn't come from us

But is
More ourselves than we are.

*

All that can be said
Of me, that I say
Myself

Of which I am,
Apparently, the cause.

*

De quoi
Ai-je peur

Sinon de moi,
Sinon de n'être plus

Qu'un moi-même abîmé?

Sinon de moi, vaincue,
Ruine de moi-même?

Mais j'en suis loin,
Je parle. Je me parle.

*

Mais oui,
Que l'on m'appelle:
Océan.

Ça me grandit
Jusqu'à moi-même.

*

Peut-être, dans tout cet espace,
D'autres océans.

Qu'est-ce que serait
Notre rencontre?

*

Of what
Am I afraid

Except of myself,
Except of existing only

As a deteriorating self?

Myself conquered,
The ruins of myself?

But that's very far away.
I talk. I talk to myself.

*

Yes.
Let them call me
Ocean.

Then I am larger
Even within myself.

*

Maybe, in all that space,
There are other oceans.

What if
We met?

*

La terre est fière
De ses couleurs.

Mais nos nuances,
À elle et à moi,

Qu'on les confronte!

*

Je ne demande rien
À quoi que ce soit.

Rien que cela:
Qu'on me laisse libre
D'être moi-même, en train

De devenir
Ce que je suis.

*

Grisaille, merveille
De mes jours, de mes nuits
Et de leurs entre-deux.

*

Moi-même, tout moi-même,
Je me sens la vague
De je ne sais quel océan.

*

The earth is proud
Of its colors.

But the shades
Of those colors and mine,

Just compare them!

*

There is nothing I ask
Of anything

Just this:
That I be left free
To be myself, in the process

Of becoming
What I am.

*

Gray light, wonder
Of my days, of my nights,
Of their in-betweens.

*

Myself, my entire self,
I feel I am the wave
Of I don't know what ocean.

*

Qui peut dire
Qu'il me lacère?

J'absorbe.

*

Curieux que là
Où plus parfaitement
Je touche mon immobilité,

Là je me sache
Mère du mouvement.

*

N'essayez pas
De me déchiffrer.

Imaginez-vous
En train de m'étreindre.

Cherchez
La méthode.

*

Who can boast
Of lacerating me?

I absorb.

*

Strange that when
I am most perfectly in touch
With my immobility,

That's when I know
I give birth to movement.

*

Don't try
To figure me out.

Imagine that you are
Holding me in your arms.

How would you
Go about it?

*

Je sens
Que j'ai une origine
Dont je ne sais rien
Ou presque—

Et c'est elle encore
Qui gouverne en moi
Quelque chose

Ou peut-être domine
Ce que je crois être.

*

On dirait
Que les vents voudraient
Que je leur conte mon histoire—

Et moi,
C'est à eux
Que je la demande.

*

L'affront de l'air.
La caresse de l'air.

*

I feel
That I have a source
About which I know almost
Nothing

And that very source
Still governs something
In me

Or perhaps has power
Over what I believe I am.

*

It seems
That the winds
Would like me to tell them my story.

And that's
Just what I ask
Of them.

*

The air taunts me.
The air caresses me.

*

Il m'arrive
D'être fatiguée des nuages—

Changeants et immuables,
Comme des adjectifs.

*

La brume
Comme essai de compromis
Entre l'air et moi.

Pour un moment,
L'horizon n'est plus.

*

J'ai observé
Le galop d'un cheval
Sur la plage.

On aurait dit
Qu'il voulait m'imiter,

Juste ce jour-là.

*

Sometimes I get
Tired of the clouds,

Shifting and inflexible,
Like adjectives.

*

Fog
An attempt at compromise
Between the air and me.

For a moment no more
Horizon.

*

I've observed
A horse galloping
On the beach.

You would have thought
He was trying to imitate me,

On that particular day.

*

Je vois sur les plages
Et sur les falaises

Des yeux qui se moquent
En me regardant.

Mais de quoi?
Pourquoi?

*

D'ailleurs, pourquoi
Me regardent-ils?

Ils n'ont donc
Pas mieux à faire?

*

Ils doivent
Regarder vers moi
Parce qu'ils croient

Qu'en moi
C'est plus simple qu'en eux.

*

I see on the beaches
And on the cliffs

Eyes
That mock me.

But what about?
Why?

*

Besides, why
Are they looking at me?

Haven't they anything
Better to do?

*

They probably
Look toward me
Because they believe

That in me
Things are simpler than in them.

*

Moi, je croirais
Volontiers le contraire,

Mais, qu'on le sache,
L'orgueil, il y a longtemps
Que j'en ai fait mon deuil.

*

Moi, je suis, simplement—
Et je ne suis pas
De ceux qui pensent.

*

Bien sûr
On peut rêver,
Rêver toujours
D'aller ailleurs,

Comme si ailleurs
N'était pas ici.

*

On peut creuser,
Aussi,

Mais creuse donc
Dans ton instant.

*

I'd be more inclined
To think the opposite.

But—I'd like this understood—
I had to give up pride
Long ago.

*

As for me, I am, simply,
And I am not
Of those who think.

*

Of course
One can dream,
Dream
Of going elsewhere,

As if elsewhere
Were somewhere else.

*

One can also
Dig.

So why don't you dig
In your own here and now.

*

Comme si chacun
De mes goémons,

Comme si même
Chacune de mes gouttes

N'était pas inépuisable—
Et qu'importe

Si ce qu'on y voit
Puisse ou non
Être comparé.

Tout
Est la même chose,

Tout
Est autre chose.

Pèse chacune
Et pèse-toi.

*

As if each one
Of my kelp fronds,

As if even
Every one of my water drops

Weren't inexhaustible –
And what does it matter

Whether or not
What one sees in them
Is comparable.

It's all
The same thing.

It's all
Something else.

Weigh each one
And weigh yourself.

*

Je finirai
Par tout avouer.

Mais alors,
Est-ce qu'il y aura
Encore une mer

Et que sera
Devenu l'alentour?

*

En attendant
On ne sait quoi,

Essayons de dormir
Et que m'épargnent
Les rêves!

*

Avant de m'endormir
Je tente de me rêver

Le contraire
De ce que je suis,

La terre à menhirs
Et à pommiers.

*

In the end,
I'll have confessed everything.

But after that
Will there still be
A sea?

And what will have happened
To its surroundings?

*

Meanwhile,
Before who-knows-what happens,

I'll try to sleep,
And may my dreams
Spare me!

*

Before falling asleep
I try to imagine myself

The opposite
Of what I am,

The land with its menhirs
And its apple trees.

*

N'ayez pas peur:
Je ne couvrirai pas,
Ne remplirai pas

Le monde.

Il y a des lois
Et je suis moi aussi
Sous leur empire.

*

J'ai donc roulé
Un tronc d'arbre
Sur la plage.

Pauvre tronc d'arbre
Et qui a cru
En mon pouvoir.

*

Il n'y a que moi
À ne pas rêver,
À ne pas vouloir

Plus de pouvoir.

C'est en moi qu'ils viennent
En crever.

*

Don't be afraid:
I won't cover,
Won't fill up

The world.

There are laws
To which I too
Submit.

*

So I rolled
A tree trunk
Up onto the beach.

Poor tree trunk –
It believed
In my power.

*

I am the only one
Who doesn't dream of,
Doesn't want

More power.

And it's into me that they come
To die of it.

*

N'empêche
Que le tronc d'arbre

Va rester,
Être là,
Sur la plage

Et gêner et appeler
Ceux qui ont
Pouvoir sur lui.

*

Je pense que le ciel,
Cet espèce de ciel,
Cette fausse couverture

Ne me contredirait pas,
Pas toujours.

Lui aussi doit s'y faire.

*

Pour lui non plus
Qui voit plus loin que moi,

Ce ne doit pas être si simple.

*

Just the same,
The tree trunk

Will stay
Right there
On the beach,

In the way and calling out
To those who have power
Over it.

*

I think the sky,
This version of the sky,
This counterfeit covering

Wouldn't contradict me,
Not always.

It too has to get used to things.

*

For it, like me,
Although it sees farther,

Things aren't so simple.

*

Pour qui d'ailleurs
Est-ce que c'est simple?

Pour la crevette?
Pour la bactérie?

Pour le plancton?

Pour quoi que ce soit
Il n'y a pas
Qu'à se laisser aller.

*

Pour le gris lui-même
C'est tout un problème
De tourner au blanc ou au noir.

Il lui arrive
De préférer rester de gris—

Mais le temps
Ne l'isole pas.

*

Calme, calme,
Comme disait l'autre,

Qui rêvait de calme
Et le cherchait dans le travail.

*

But is there anyone
For whom they are simple?

For the shrimp?
For the bacterium?

For the plankton?

For whatever it is
There's nothing to do
But go along.

*

For grey
It's very hard
To avoid turning white or black.

Sometimes it would prefer
Just to be grey

But time
Won't isolate it.

*

Calm, calm,
As the other one used to say,

The one who dreamed of calm
And sought it in work.

*

On dit: je m'efface.
On dit: je m'enfonce—

Et on est là.

*

Et si quand même
Il arrivait

Qu'il n'y ait plus que moi
Sur cette boule,

Que moi et plus rien
À quoi me heurter,
Où me reposer?

Sur moi
Plus aucun regard?

*

People say: I withdraw,
People say: I sink down

And there we are.

*

And if, just the same,
It happened

That I was the only one left
On this sphere.

Just me and nothing
To fling myself against,
Where could I rest?

Without anyone
To look at me?

*

À ce que je vois,
L'arbre au moins
Se divise en branches

Et elles
En rameaux, en feuilles,
En chatons,

Mais moi
Je ne peux qu'en rêver.

*

Un enfant
M'a jeté une rose.

Je suis loin
D'en avoir fini
Avec elle,

Qui me cache tout.

*

Pouvoir, pouvoir,
On ne rêve que de ça—

Moi, par exemple
De faire du plancton
Avec les rochers.

*

It seems
That the trees, at least,
Divide themselves into branches

And these
Into twigs, leaves,
Buds,

But that
I can only dream about.

*

A child
Threw me a rose.

It will be a long time
Before I'm finished
With that flower

Which refuses to tell me anything.

*

Power, power,
What everyone dreams of

Including me,
Wanting to make plankton
Out of rocks.

*

Que je me répète,
C'est évident.

Je me répète en parlant
Comme en ne faisant rien,

En étant ici,
En étant là,

En étant.

*

Si je ne me répétais pas,
Qu'est-ce que je ferais?

Je répète
Mon existence.

*

Je dois bien constater
Que quand je bouge fort

Je fais de l'écume
Et qu'elle est d'un blanc
Qui ne me convient guère,

D'un blanc pareil à celui
Que portent les nuages
Assez souvent.

*

I repeat myself,
That's obvious.

I repeat myself when I talk
And when I'm doing nothing,

When I am here,
When I am there,

When I am.

*

If I didn't repeat myself,
What would I do?

I repeat
My existence.

*

I can't help noticing
That when I move a lot

I make foam
Whose whiteness
Is inappropriate.

A whiteness like the one
Clouds wear
Quite often.

*

Il y a des endroits sur la planète
Où je suis sans marées,

Mais là, j'en fais autant qu'ailleurs,
Dans mes intérieurs.

*

Plages, grèves, rivages
Largement s'étendent

Pour que je les caresse
Longuement.

*

Lorsque je pense à moi,
C'est toujours en un point
Où je suis toute entière

Ramassée. Rayonnant.

*

Les plages ne brillent
Que lorsque d'elles je viens
De me retirer.

*

There are places on the planet
Where I don't have any tides,
I make just as many there as anywhere,
Within myself.

*

Beaches, shores, riverbanks
Stretch out as widely as they can

For me to caress
At length.

*

When I think about myself,
It's always at one point
Which contains me totally

Gathered together. Radiant.

*

Beaches only shine
When I have just
Left them.

*

Pour moi
La différence

Entre un nageur
Et un noyé:

Je sens que le noyé
Ne me craint plus.

*

Les vagues
Ont bien quelque tendance
À s'individualiser,

Mais elles me rejoignent
Assez vite ou bien

Se séparent de moi pour de bon
Et meurent d'évaporation.

*

Tout passe, tout casse, tout lasse,
N'est-ce pas?

Sauf moi.

*

For me
Here's the difference

Between someone drowned
And a swimmer:

The drowned
Are no longer afraid.

*

The waves may tend
To stand out
As individuals,

But they come back to me
Quite soon or else

Leave me altogether,
And die of evaporation.

*

Nothing lasts, fading fast, soon past—
Right!

Except me.

*

Normalement,
Dit-on,

Mais qu'est-ce
Qui peut être normal

Dans un monde où j'existe?

*

Si je me laissais
Aller au lyrisme,

Je pourrais m'admirer
Impunément.

*

Ce qui me fait trembler
Ce n'est pas la tempête.

Elle ne concerne guère
Que ma surface.

Je tremble de savoir
Que je vais durer,

Alors que sur les terres
Autour de moi,

Tout naît, grandit et meurt,
Même les rochers.

*

Normally,
They say.

But can anything
Be normal

In a world where I exist?

*

If I let myself
Be lyrical

I could admire myself
With impunity.

*

What makes me tremble
Is not the storm

Which only concerns
My surface.

I tremble at the thought
That I'm going to last

While in all the lands
Around me,

Everything is born, grows up, and dies,
Even the rocks.

*

Je devrai donc toujours
Voir mourir les autres

Et n'aurai pas le temps
De faire une amitié
Qui traverse les siècles.

*

Je ne cache pas que j'ai plaisir
À me sentir envahie, pénétrée
Par les eaux des fleuves.

Elles m'apportent le goût
Des choses de la terre.

*

Il m'arrive
Dans mes intérieurs

De me bercer
Longuement, doucement,

Jusqu'à ne plus avoir envie
Que de me retenir,
De me reposer.

*

So I will always have to
See the others die

And won't have time
To create a friendship
That would outlast the centuries.

*

I don't deny that I enjoy
Feeling myself invaded, penetrated
By the water of rivers.

They bring me the taste
Of terrestrial things.

*

Sometimes,
Deep inside,

I rock myself gently,
For a long time,

Until my only desire
Is to hold myself back,
And rest.

*

Je m'étonne

Qu'étant donné ce que je sais,
Connaissant mon volume,
Ma pesanteur, ma puissance
De résistance,

Par moments je me sente fragile,
À la merci
D'une piqûre d'épine.

*

Je passe des années
À me répéter:

Moi, silence,
Moi, silence.

*

Je n'étreins pas les bateaux,
Qu'ils naviguent ou qu'ils coulent.

Je n'étreins pas les baleines,
Les poissons,
Le soleil couchant.

Je n'étreins
Que mon souci d'éternité.

*

It astonishes me

That in spite of all I know about
My volume,
My weight, my power
Of resistance,

There are moments when I feel fragile,
Vulnerable
To the prick of a thorn.

*

I spend years
Repeating to myself:

I, silence,
I, silence.

*

I don't embrace the boats
Sailing along or sinking.

I don't embrace the whales,
The fish,
The setting sun.

I only embrace
My concern about eternity.

*

La lune, oui,
La lune m'aspire
Un peu, si peu—
Et me rejette.

Jamais
Nous ne nous rejoindrons.

*

Ce qu'ils appellent
Un raz-de-marée,

Ce qui leur fait
Tellement peur,

C'est bien peu pour moi.

*

Ces hommes qui me regardent
Jusqu'à s'oublier

Souffrent
De n'être pas
Ce que je suis pour eux.

*

The moon, yes,
The moon breathes me upward
A little, so little,
And then rejects me.

Never
Will we be together.

*

What they call
A tidal wave,

Something that
Terrifies them,

I scarcely notice.

*

Those who look at me so long
They forget about themselves

Suffer
Because they are not
What I am for them.

*

Je ne parlerai pas
Aux couleurs.

J'en vois sur les côtes
Qui me regardent.

Est-ce à moi qu'elles racontent
Un devenir chargé d'une histoire
Aussi vieille que la mienne?

Je les comprends
Sans comprendre.

*

Je sens
Que loin, très loin dans les terres,

Des hommes s'endorment
En se laissant
Bercer par moi.

*

I won't talk
To the colors.

I see them on the coasts
Looking at me.

Is it to me that they tell about
The weight they carry with them
Of a story as old as mine?

I understand them
Without understanding.

*

I can feel
That in lands very far away,

People fall asleep
Letting themselves
Be rocked by me.

*

J'ai beau me redire:
"Ne reste pas toujours à regarder le ciel

Dont tu fais les nuages
Et qui reste étranger,
Voué à qui sait quoi,

Occupe-toi plutôt
Des profondeurs qui sont les tiennes."

Je dois bien constater ce besoin qui me point
De ce qui n'est pas moi,
Que je rêve de caresser.

*

Ce besoin, c'est aussi
De me renseigner sur moi,

Et là plus que le ciel
Les côtes me sont utiles

Avec leurs maisons,
Leurs prés, leurs champs,
Leurs habitants, leurs arbres,

Même les routes.

*

There's no point in my repeating to myself:
"Why must you be always looking at the sky

And making clouds –
It's not of your kind,
And who knows what it cares about?

Your business is with the depths
Which are your own."

I'm well aware of my painful need
For what is not myself,
And that I long to caress.

*

That is also a need
To learn about myself,

And more useful than the sky
Are the coasts

With their houses,
Their meadows, their fields,
Their people, their trees,

Even the roads.

*

Je me renseigne
En me comparant à eux

Ou bien c'est eux qui parlent
En se comparant à moi.

Quelle différence y a-t-il?

Nous ne sommes pas
Et nous sommes
Du même réseau.

*

Eux, sur la côte,
Ils sont plus sûrs que moi
D'eux-mêmes,

Puisqu'ils ont de la solidité,
Des formes, qu'ils offrent
Une résistance au vent,
À la lumière—

Et pourtant moi
Je ne périclite pas.

*

I learn
By comparing myself to them

Or else they are the ones who talk,
Comparing themselves to me.

What difference does it make?

We are not
And we are
On the same network.

*

They, on the coast,
Are more sure of themselves
Than I am,

Because they have solid
Forms that offer
Resistance to the wind,
And to light—

But just the same, I
Don't collapse.

*

Peut-être
Que ceux de la côte et moi

Nous passons notre temps
À essayer de trouver le code
Qui régirait nos rapports,

Mais peut-être ce code
Est-il toujours là,
Au fond du silence.

*

Sauf les jours d'orage
(D'où viennent les orages?)

Toutes ces choses
Que je vois sur la terre

Ont plutôt l'air bon enfant,

Et peut-être
Que cet air ne ment pas.

*

It may be
That those on the coast and I

Spend our time
Trying to establish laws
That would govern our relationship,

But perhaps those laws
Are already in place,
In the depths of silence.

*

Except on stormy days
(Where do storms come from?)

All those things
That I see on land

Appear rather friendly,

And perhaps
Those appearances do not lie.

*

Je me veux
Et me crois innocente.

Mais ces requins,
Alors,

D'où viennent-ils?
Qui les a faits?

*

Je dis
Que je ne suis pas violente, moi,

Que mes colères
Ne sont pas les miennes,

Que ce sont celles
Du soleil et du vent.

Mais reste à savoir
Si je n'y suis pas pour quelque chose,

Reste à savoir si parfois
Il n'y a pas en moi
Un appel vers eux

Pour que ça me prenne.

*

I want to be,
And believe I am, innocent.

But what about
Those sharks

Where do they come from?
Who created them?

*

I say
That I personally am not violent,

That my rages
Aren't really mine,

They belong to
The sun and the wind.

But it remains to be seen
If I'm not involved in it too,

It remains to be seen
If there isn't something in me
That may call out to them

On purpose.

*

Si je me fais silence,
Regardant dehors
Ou ne regardant pas,

C'est pour m'écouter,
Pour m'écouter en moi,
Pas pour entendre quelque chose

Qui viendrait du dehors.

*

Besoin de me dire
Que toujours moi, la mer,
Serai la plus grande,

Plus grande
Que n'importe
Quelle immensité

*

Vous n'en aurez jamais fini
Avec moi,

Avec mes diverses
Monotonies.

*

If I become silence,
Looking outside
Or not looking,

It's to listen to myself,
Listen to the self within myself,
Not to hear something

Which would come from the outside.

*

That need to tell myself
That I, the sea,
Will always be the biggest,

Bigger
Than any other
Immensity.

*

You will never come to the end
Of me,

And my various
Monotonies.

*

Pauvre montagne,
Tu n'as pas

Autant que moi
De divertissements.

*

Il m'arrive de regretter
De n'être pas forcée
Par plus puissant que moi,

De regarder sur la terre
Un point fixe,
Toujours le même,
De le regarder
Un long moment,
Au moins de temps en temps.

*

Et si je me dressais
Une fois, tout à coup,
À la verticale,

Tendant vers l'espace,
Tendant vers tous

Mes bas-fonds avec qui
Moi-même je vis peu.

*

Poor mountain,
You haven't as many

Sources of entertainment
As I do.

*

Sometimes I regret
Not being forced
By some superior power

To look at one fixed point
On land
Always the same one,

To look at it
A long while,
At least from time to time.

*

If I stood straight up,
All at once,
Vertical

Extending into space
Extending toward everyone

My lower depths
With which I myself am little acquainted.

*

J'ai quelque mal
À me sentir
La partie d'une boule.

*

Des gens me regardent
Comme s'ils attendaient

Voir de moi
Sortir le temps.

*

Parfois,
Je ne suis qu'un rêve,

Il me semble
Que quelqu'un ou quelque chose
Me rêve

Et je sens
Qu'il en souffre

Et moi-même
Je souffre en lui.

*

It's difficult for me
To feel that I'm
Part of a sphere.

*

People look at me
As if they were expecting

To see time itself
Rising out of me.

*

Sometimes,
I am only a dream,

It seems to me
That someone or something
Dreams me,

And I feel
His suffering

And my own suffering
Within him.

*

Le bleu du jour,
L'or et la pourpre du soir,
C'est pour moi—

Qui n'y suis pour rien
Que pour saluer,

Regretter, attendre
Ou tâcher
De n'y plus penser.

*

Est-ce que le regard
Que je porte vers mes intérieurs

Est le même que celui
Que j'essaie de poser
Sur les extérieurs?

*

La ressemblance
Entre la houle
Qui remue les feuilles des arbres

Et celle qui remue mon eau.

*

The blue of daytime,
The gold and crimson of evening,
It's for me—

And all I can do
Is acknowledge,

Regret, wait,
Or try
Not to think about it.

*

When I look
Toward my interiors,

Is it the same look
As when I try to see
The exteriors?

*

The similarity
Between the wind storm
That moves the leaves of trees

And the ground-swell that moves my water.

*

La différence
Entre les pigeons des arbres

Et les mouettes
Sur mes confins.

*

Les uns et les autres
Ont pourtant un cri

Que renient le merle
Et le rossignol.

*

Nuages, nuages,
Mes fils
Aux allures de courtisans.

*

Et si ce n'était
Que le temps lui-même
Qui me rêve

Comme peut-être il rêve
Toutes les choses?

*

The difference
Between the pigeons in the trees

And the seagulls
Around my edges.

*

Both of them, however,
Have a cry

That blackbirds
And nightingales disavow.

*

Clouds, clouds,
My sons
With the bearing of courtesans.

*

And it could be only
Time itself
Which dreams me

As perhaps it dreams
All things?

*

Bien sûr,
Si je me laissais aller

Je penserais
Que c'est le néant qui me rêve—

Alors que ce qui n'est pas
Ne doit pas avoir pouvoir
De rêver.

*

Ce sera donc
Mon pouvoir à moi
De rêver

Que le néant me rêve—

Et c'est pourquoi
J'ai ce malaise.

*

Peut-être que la lumière
Ne vient pas du soleil,

Que le soleil ne vient
Que pour voir cette lumière

Que tous ensemble
Et les uns contre les autres
Nous émettons.

*

Of course,
If I let myself go,

I would think
That it's nothingness which dreams me—

Yet how could what is not
Have the power
To dream?

*

So it's within
My own power
To dream

That I'm the dream of nothingness—

That's why
I'm so uneasy.

*

Maybe light
Doesn't come from the sun

And the sun only comes
To see that light

That all of us
Pressed close together
Emit.

*

Monstre que tu es,
Me crie-t-on parfois.

Je manque d'éléments
Pour en juger,

Mais volontiers
Je le crois:

Je suis un monstre.
Je suis un monstre.

*

Mais qu'est-ce
Qui n'est pas un monstre

De tout cela
Que je vois ou devine?

Un monstre, cet azur,
Un monstre, ce clocher.

*

"Monster that you are!"
People shout at me sometimes.

I haven't the means
To evaluate that

But I'm ready
To believe it:

I'm a monster.
I'm a monster.

*

But what
Isn't a monster

Of all that
I see or sense?

A monster, that blue sky,
A monster, that steeple.

*

Qu'est-ce qui n'est pas un monstre
Quand on l'attaque,

Quand on réveille
Ses profondeurs?

Déchirez donc l'azur
Et vous verrez.

Caressez le soleil à rebrousse-poil
Et vous verrez.

*

En toute chose
Le monstre est plus ou moins visible.

Il est même possible
Que moi, ce soit au repos
Que j'inquiète le plus,

Que les terrifie tous
Ma lassitude

Ou le désir
De ne vivre que moi.

*

What isn't a monster
When it's attacked,

When its depths
Are awakened?

Rip that blue sky
And you'll see,

Stroke the sun in the wrong direction
And you'll see.

*

In all things
The monster is more or less visible.

In my case, it's even possible
That I cause the most worry
When I'm at rest,

That my lassitude
Terrifies everyone

Or my desire
To live nothing but my life.

*

Tellement je le sens,
Je le vis
Ce pin sur mes bords,

Que je finis par croire
Que c'est moi qui le fais,
Que c'est en moi qu'il dure.

*

Un cri
Jeté contre moi
Reste un cri.

*

Il paraît
Qui j'ai une odeur
Et qu'elle est forte.

Ça doit être celle
Des temps accumulés

À travers
Les origines successives.

*

So intensely do I feel it
That I live
That pine tree on my shore,

Believing, in the end,
That I am its creator,
That it lives its life in me.

*

A cry
Hurled against me
Remains a cry.

*

Apparently
I smell of something
Strong.

It must be from
The accumulation of time

Through
Successive beginnings.

*

Je me demande
Si ce que je me marmonne

À longueur de temps,
À longueur de marées

Ne serait pas un chant.

*

Je me demande
Si ce rocher est à sa place.

*

Un jour, aussi bien,
Je me réveillerai soleil.

*

Que rien
Ne puisse m'humilier!

Que rien
Ne puisse me blesser!

Rien que moi
Si je m'y mettais.

I wonder
If all my muttering

The length of time
The length of tides

Isn't a song.

*

I wonder
If that rock is in the right place.

*

Some day, I could just as well
Wake up as a sun.

*

May nothing have the power
To humiliate me!

May nothing have the power
To hurt me!

Only myself
If I really tried.

from MAINTENANT (NOW)
(1993)

On veut toujours
Aller au-delà.

Au-delà de quoi,
On ne sait pas.

Au-delà
De ce qui est en soi?

Au-delà
De ce qui n'y est pas?

Au-delà de quelque chose
Qui n'existe pas?

We always want
To go beyond.

Beyond what
We don't know.

Beyond
What is within us?

Beyond
What isn't there?

Beyond something
That doesn't exist?

Vieillir
A dit à la rose le vent.

Tu sais: bientôt
Quand je passerai par là
Je n'aurai plus tes pétales
A caresser.

Mais moi-même,
Qu'en sera-t-il de moi?

Growing old
The wind said to the rose.

Soon, you know,
When I pass by,
I'll no longer have your petals
To caress.

But what about me?
What will I be then?

Quand il ne se passe rien
Et que tu penses
Qu'il ne se passe rien,

Il se passe bien
Que tu penses
Que rien ne se passe.

Cela pèse alors
Comme un événement,

Où le temps sur lui-même
Se concentre—

Et tu fais comme lui.

When nothing is happening
And you are thinking
That nothing is happening,

What is happening
Is that you are thinking
That nothing is happening,

Which then has the weight
Of an event,

In which time concentrates
On itself—

Just as you are doing.

Tu n'as pas réussi
A faire de tous les instants de ta vie
Un miracle?

Essaie encore.

You haven't succeeded
In making every instant of your life
A miracle?

Try again.

Je ne suis pas à moi,
Mais à l'univers

Et sur celui-ci
J'ai peu de pouvoir

Quand tout ce qui existe
A pouvoir sur moi,

Presque toujours
Sans se faire connaître.

I don't belong to myself.
I belong to the universe

Over which
I haven't much power

While everything that exists
Has power over me,

Almost always
Without introducing itself.

L'espace attire,
Fait peur.

On ne sait jamais bien
Si l'on en a trop
Ou pas assez.

On le fuit,
On l'attaque.

Le mieux
Est d'essayer de se tailler
L'espace de sa propre sphère,

Dans ce royaume
Ami et plus ou moins soumis—

Avec comme perspective
De parfois s'offrir à l'espace.

Space attracts,
Frightens.

We never know
Whether we have too much,
Or not enough.

We flee it,
We attack it.

Best
To try to carve out
The space of your own sphere,

In that kingdom, fricndly,
And more or less subdued—

With the occasional prospect
Of giving itself to space.

Si tu venais tout près de moi,
Belle mésange,

Et que nous nous regardions
Comme font le ciel
Et la forêt,

Sans penser à rien d'autre
Qu'à ce regard,

Alors, je trouverais peut-être
A me dire, m'entendre dire

Le secret que je cherche en moi
Depuis toujours.

You, lovely bluebird,
If you came really close to me

And we looked at each other
The way the sky and the forest
Look at each other

Thinking of nothing
But what is before our eyes,

Then perhaps I would find the way
To tell myself, hear myself tell,

The secret that all my life
I've been searching for from within.

Quelle danse
Nous avons ensemble dansée,

Cette roche et moi,
L'un dans l'autre,

Je ne sais combien de temps
A la frontière de l'éternité,

A la limite indécise
Entre la pierre et la chair.

Et depuis,
Lequel des deux pourrait dire

Qu'il est plus que l'autre
Offert à leur antique secret?

What a dance
We danced together

That rock and I,
One inside the other,

For I don't know how long
On the edge of eternity,

On the hesitating border
Between stone and flesh.

And since then,
Which one of us could claim

To be, more than the other,
Offered up to their secret of old?

Peu de chose
Est ce que tu vois.

Peu de chose
Tout ce que tu devines.

Pourtant
Le sentiment

D'être le régisseur
De ta durable joie.

You don't see
Very much.

You don't sense
Very much.

And yet
This feeling

Of being in control
Of your lasting joy.

—Qu'est-ce que tu attends
A la fenêtre,
Tout tendu on dirait,
Vers quoi?

—Je n'attends rien.
Je n'observe rien.
Je vois sans regarder.

—Mais si tu attends,
Tu attends quelque chose,
Tu attends l'effraction en toi
De maintenant.

Ohrid, août 1986—
Belley, août 1992.

—What are you waiting for,
Standing at the window?
You seem all intent
On something outside.

—I'm not waiting for anything.
I'm not observing anything.
I see without looking.

—But I know that you are waiting,
Waiting for something,
Waiting to be invaded
By the now.

Ohrid, August 1986 –
Belley, August 1992

from PRÉSENT (PRESENT)
(1987–97)

Si je ne regarde plus le ravin,
Si je lui tourne le dos,
Si je m'en vais,

Déjà je sais
Que je vais l'entendre
Lancer un appel—

Et que faire?

05.01.87

If I stop looking at the ravine,
If I turn my back on it,
If I go away,

I know in advance
That I'll hear it
Call out to me—

And then what?

5/01/87

Les choses
Qui sont autour de moi

Laissent entendre:
Je ne dirai rien.

Pourtant, c'est comme si
Elles me parlaient.

30.01.87–02.02.87

The things
Around me

Mutely
Refuse to speak.

And yet, it seems
They are talking to me.

30/01/87–02/02/87

Quand voici que c'est l'aube,

Est-ce le soleil
Qui honore la terre

Ou la terre
Qui honore le soleil?

29.04.87

When suddenly dawn appears,

Is it the sun
Honoring the earth,

Or the earth
Honoring the sun?

29/04/87

Regarde-toi
Dans la glace.

Regarde-toi bien
Et constate:

Plus tu te regardes
Moins tu te vois.

13.02.88

Look at yourself
In the mirror.

Take a good look
And notice

That the more you look at yourself,
The less of your self do you see.

13/02/88

Je regarde un rocher.
Il est ce que je vois,

Il est aussi
Ce que je ne vois pas,

Mais cela
Je le sens,

Je le vois
Plus ou moins bien

Avec et à travers
Ce que je vois.

11.10.88

I look at a rock.
It is what I see.

It is also
What I don't see.

But that
I sense

I see
More or less well

With and through
What I see.

11/10/88

Pourquoi parler aux pierres?
Elles ne répondent pas.

Quand j'étais enfant
Elles me répondaient
Par la mer.

Aujourd'hui,
Imaginer
Ne suffit pas.

30.12.93

Why talk to stones?
They don't answer.

When I was a child,
They answered me
Through the sea.

Now,
Imagining
Isn't enough.

30/12/93

La poésie, c'est la recherche
Passionnelle et comblée

De quelque chose que l'on sait
Ne jamais atteindre.

01.01.95

Poetry is the impassioned
Fulfilling search

For something you know
Is forever out of reach.

01.01.95

Question:
Sait-on se donner

Entièrement
À ce que l'on écrit?

Écrire ainsi
Est une forme de l'amour

Dont on cherche à deviner
Ce qui l'inspire.

Et tu ne devineras pas d'avance.
À toi de trouver en écrivant.

10.09.96

Question:
Is it possible to give yourself

Totally
To what you write?

To write that way
Is a form of love

Not knowing
What has inspired it.

And you won't find out in advance.
Up to you to find out as you write.

10/09/96

from POSSIBLES FUTURS (POSSIBLE FUTURES) (1996)

DU SILENCE

Je fore,
Je creuse.

Je fore
Dans le silence

Ou plutôt
Dans du silence,

Celui qu'en moi
Je fais.

Et je fore, je creuse
Vers plus de silence,

Vers le grand,
Le total silence en ma vie

Où le monde, je l'espère,
Me révélera quelque chose de lui.

SILENCE

I drill,
I dig.

I drill
Into silence

Not silence itself
But that silence

I create
In myself.

And I drill, I dig
Toward increasing silence,

Toward the great,
The total silence within my life

Where the world, I hope,
Will reveal to me something of itself.

Je veux entrer
Mais je ne sais
Ni où ni dans quoi.

Il semblerait que ce soit là
Où je me confondrais

Avec la source de ce
Dont j'ai toujours eu besoin.

I want to enter
But I don't know
How or into what.

It seems to me that there
I would merge

With the source of whatever it is
I have always needed.

Mon royaume
C'est du silence

Où je ne règne pas,
Je ne régente pas.

Je le laisse me posséder.
Je l'aide en cela
Par tout ce qui me crée.

Je me baigne en lui
Comme si je le touchais
Par quelque chose en moi

Dont je ne connais
Que l'existence

Et ce que de l'immensité
Il assigne à mon désir.

My kingdom
Consists of a silence

I do not rule
Nor command.

I let it possess me,
I help it to do so
With all that brings me into being.

I float within the silence,
Touching it
Through something in me

About which I only know
That it exists

And how much immensity
It bestows on my desire.

C'est le silence
Qui m'apporte, qui me donne
Le souffle du monde.

Il me permet
De me connaître en lui

À l'écoute
De mon être
Tel que je le pressens.

Il m'ouvre une porte
Sur un espace de calme

Où s'éclaire la présence
Indispensable.

It is silence
Which brings to me, lets me feel,
The breathing of the world.

Allowing me
To know myself within it

Alert
For my being
I know I would recognize.

Silence opens a door
Into a space where calm

Illuminates
The indispensable presence.

Dans mon royaume
Je sens soudain passer par moi

Le constant croisement
De l'espace et du temps.

In my kingdom
Suddenly I feel passing through me

The constant intersection
Of space and time.

Mon royaume de silence
A la forme d'une sphère.

Je n'y suis pas au centre
Mais quelque part en haut.

Là où je me tiens
Tout me revient, tout m'arrive.

J'ausculte
Un présent sans frontière.

My kingdom of silence
Is shaped like a sphere.

I am not in its center
But somewhere up above.

There, in the place I hold,
Everything comes back, everything reaches me,

I press my ear
To a borderless present.

Je me vis au plein
De la sphère de silence

Que je parviens
Même parfois dans les bruits,

À créer autour de moi
Tellement mon être

Sait donner de lui-même
Pour créer le royaume

Où je communie
Avec la teneur de ce silence,

Avec sa sève
Qui est aussi la mienne.

I live my life at the core
Of the sphere of silence

Which sometimes,
Even in noisy places,

I can create around me,
So much will my being

Give of itself
To create that kingdom

Where I am one
With the fabric of this silence,

With its sap,
Which is also mine.

Est-ce que l'océan
Dans ses profondeurs

Possède autant de silence
Que j'en ai en moi?

Sinon, est-ce
Pour se libérer de son bruit

Qu'il vient sur nos côtes
Faire tout ce tapage

Ravager ce qu'il peut
Pour enfin s'affaler

Comme sur un lit
Fait de douceur?

Does the ocean
Hold in its depths

As much silence
As I have in myself?

If not, is it
To escape its own noises

That it comes roaring
Onto our shores

Doing all the damage it can
Before collapsing

As onto a bed
Of pure softness?

Dans mon royaume,
Pas d'arbres, pas de maisons,

Que le silence
Et ce qu'il m'encourage

À lui apporter par ma présence,
Mon désir.

Nous restons ainsi
À jouir l'un de l'autre

Comme font le ciel
Et sa charge d'azur.

In my kingdom
There are no houses, no trees,

Only silence
And what it asks for:

The gift of my presence
My desire.

So we remain
Delighting in each other

Like the sky
And its charge of blue.

Dans mon royaume
Une rivière
Coule très lentement

Elle ne fait aucun bruit,
Se promet à l'éternité.

Through my kingdom
A river
Very slowly flows,

Soundless,
Vowed to eternity.

Je pénètre souvent
Dans mon royaume

Avec une femme, ma femme,
La dame du silence,

Ensemble nous goûtons
Chacun notre bonheur

En même temps
Que celui du silence complice.

Et dans ces heures-là
Le royaume se rêve

Et se retrouve
Bénissant.

I often make my way
Into my kingdom

With a woman, my wife,
The lady of silence;

Together we each enjoy
Our happiness

As does silence
In its complicity.

And in those moments
The kingdom becomes its own dream

And finds itself
A blessing.

Tant d'années,
Tant de douleurs, de joies
Et de vacance en dehors de tout

M'ont permis de m'acharner
À créer le royaume
Où je m'englobe.

Là, je convoque
La fleur que je choisis

Pour la vivre, me fortifier.

Et vient le moment
Où la fleur se fane,
Prépare sa résurrection.

So many years,
So much suffering, and joy,
And just beyond everything, nothing,

Have allowed me to use all my strength
To create the kingdom
Where I take my place.

There I summon
The chosen flower

To make it my life, grow stronger.

And, when the time comes
For the flower to fade,
Prepare its resurrection.

Des pensées, des souvenirs
Pas toujours faciles

À chasser, à guérir
Viennent troubler le royaume.

Alors, envahi
J'abandonne le poiein.

Je m'occupe.
Je me laisse habiter

Par un quotidien
Qui m'absorbe—

Jusqu'à ce que le royaume
Revienne me prendre.

Thoughts, memories,
Not always easy

To dispel or to heal,
Invade the peace of the kingdom.

Then, overcome,
I put my work away.

I busy myself.
I let myself be possessed

By the everyday
Which absorbs me—

Until the kingdom
Takes me back again.

Les bruits? les vaincre,
Les éloigner, les oublier,

C'est tout mon savoir
D'éteignoir de bruits.

Je puise
Dans ma réserve de force
Au fond de moi-même.

Je ne gagne pas toujours.
Aux abords du royaume,
Je résiste.

Noises? Conquer them,
Make them withdraw, forget them.

Those are all my skills
As a noise extinguisher.

I draw on
Reserves of strength
I keep in my depths.

I may not prevail.
Close to the kingdom, sometimes,
I resist.

Bonheur de constater
Que dans ma sphère

Silence et joie
Se confondent.

What happiness to perceive
That within my sphere

Silence and joy
Merge.

C'est comme si
La longue plongée dans le silence
Me lavait, me purifiait,

Effaçant sur moi
Les taches que font
Les heures sans intérêt,

Ces heures vides
Où pour tenir on cherche
À quoi s'accrocher,

Où parfois la fatigue
Oblige à s'arrêter.

It's as if
My long dive into silence
Had washed me, purified me,

Cleansed my skin
Of the stains
From hours without purpose,

Those empty hours
When we feel the need
Of something to cling to,

When sometimes we are so tired
We have to stop.

Plus facile de trouver
Son royaume de silence
Dans la solitude et l'immobilité

Que dans la foule
Et le vagabondage,

Mais c'est parfois possible.
La condition:

Le don total
De soi-même à soi.

Easier to find
A kingdom of silence
In solitude and immobility

Than in crowds
And aimless wandering,

But sometimes it is possible.
One condition:

That you give yourself completely
To yourself.

Tout ce que je fais apparaître
Dans mon silence

Est prêt à se donner
Avec un sourire
Porteur du bonheur de silence.

Whatever I cause to appear
Within my silence

Is ready to give itself
With a smile that carries
The happiness of silence.

Le bonheur
Dans mon royaume de silence

C’est de communier
Avec soi-même
En toute chose.

Happiness
In my kingdom of silence

Is to be as one
With oneself
In everything.

Je me dis que la prune
Vit en son noyau

Comme je vis en moi
Dans le sanctuaire

De mon royaume.

It seems to me that a plum
Lives within its stone

As I live within myself
In the sanctuary

Of my kingdom.

Dans mon royaume
Rien ne me pèse
Mais tout a son poids.

C'est comme si ma joie
Délivrait chaque chose
De sa pesanteur

Et me l'apportait
Tel un cadeau
Que me ferait l'espace.

In my kingdom
Nothing weighs on me
But everything has weight.

It's as if my joy
Brought lightness
To all things

And each one
Was a gift
Offered to me by space.

Dans mon royaume
Une feuille d'arbre
Est une feuille.

Je n'opte jamais
Pour l'immensité—

Je suis moi-même petit.

Et pourtant il me semble
Que tout le souffle qui cherche
À faire vivre le monde
Je le retrouve ici

Où toute chose
Avec moi communie.

In my kingdom
A leaf from a tree
Is a leaf.

I never seek
Immensity—

I myself am small.

And yet it seems to me
That from here
Comes the breath
Which brings the world to life,

From here where all things
Are at one with me.

Quand vers le haut
J'ouvre mon royaume,
Rien ne trouble mon silence.

Le ciel est toujours
D'un azur un peu pâle
Qui paraît me faire entendre:

Aime-toi un peu plus,
Quand même.

When I open my kingdom
Upward
Nothing disturbs my silence.

The blue of the sky is always
A little pale
And seems to be telling me:

Give yourself a little more love,
Just the same.

Il m'arrive parfois
De faire entrer
Dans mon royaume
Un oiseau
Et je le fais chanter.

Toujours il me chante
Des airs que je ne connais pas
Mais qui m'agréent,
M'expriment
Le centre du royaume,

Le renouvellent,
Me l'approprient davantage,
Me donnent aussi
Envie de chanter—
Et je chante.

It happens sometimes
That I invite
Into my kingdom
A bird
And I ask it to sing.

It always sings
Tunes I've not heard before
Which please me
And tell me
Of the center of the kingdom,

Make it more vivid,
More my own,
And make me
Want to sing too,
And I do sing.

Je sais parler
Au rossignol.

La preuve:
Il me répond

Et son chant
Entre dans mon royaume,

Nourrit le silence.

I know how to talk
To nightingales.

The proof:
They answer me

And their singing
Penetrates my kingdom,

Feeds the silence.

Comme tous les royaumes,
Mon royaume n'est pas
À l'abri des menaces:

Tantôt il disparaît,
Tantôt il m'expulse.

Reste à le reconquérir,
À le mériter, à se mériter.

Nécessité de rassembler en soi
Toutes les provinces de silence,

D'en créer
Parfois contre ce qui veut
S'installer en moi.

Nécessité de se retrouver.

Like all kingdoms
My kingdom is not,
Protected from threats.

Sometimes it disappears,
Sometimes it casts me out.

I have to conquer it again,
Deserve it, deserve who I am.

I need to gather within myself
All the provinces of silence,

Creating them sometimes
Against what seeks
To install itself in me,

I need to come back to myself.

Je sens que le lac
Doit vivre son eau

Comme je vis le silence
Dans mon royaume,

Qu'il se possède lui aussi
Au long des heures,

Mais lui, sait-il
Qu'il a été mon maître

Dans l'art d'épouser le temps
Au sein du silence?

I sense that the lake
Lives its water

As I live the silence
In my kingdom,

That the lake too is self-possessed,
Hour after hour,

But does the lake know
That it has taught me

How to make a spouse of time
In the heart of silence?

Que viens-tu faire, poème,
Dans le royaume?

Je viens pour approfondir
Le silence,

Pour t'emmener au plus pur de lui,
Là où il te fait vivre

L'espérance que le monde
A de son avenir, là

Où il trouve
Ce que tu attends de lui et de toi:

La fusion.

Poem, what are you doing
In the kingdom?

I've come to explore the depths
Of the silence,

To bring you to the purest of itself,
Where you learn to live

The world's hope
For its future, there

Where it discovers
What you expect of it and of yourself:

Fusion.

Bonheur
De se voir arrivé
Au centre du royaume.

Alors, on écoute
Tout en regardant

Une lumière
Éprise d'elle-même

Qui nous porte
Le silence et moi.

Happiness
To know that I have come
To the center of the kingdom.

There one can listen
And also look

As light
Delights in itself

Carrying the silence
Carrying me.

Repos. Repos.

Contemplation
De la lumière

Qui est en moi,
En dehors de moi,

La même lumière
Qui fraternise

Avec elle-même,
Avec moi.

Le silence, ma lumière,
Est devenu joie.

1994

Rest. Rest.

Contemplation
Of the light

Which is in me,
Outside me,

The same light
Which is a friend

To itself
To me.

Now, in the silence,
That light is joy.

1994

The Life & Works of Guillevic: A Chronology

1907:	August 5, birth of Eugène Alphonse Marie GUILLEVIC in Carnac, Venelle de la Forge.
1909:	His father, first a seaman, enters the national military police corps and leaves Carnac for Jeumont (Northen France) where he is apppointed and takes the family.
1912:	Moves back to Brittany in Saint Jean Brévelay (Morbihan). The family lives in the police quarters.
1912–19:	During the holidays at his mother's family village near Carnac the young child experiences intense moments of freedom and joy. The megaliths and the sea will impregnate his thoughts forever.
1919:	Departure for Ferrette, Upper Rhine.
1920–25:	High School in Altkirch (Alsatia) where he must learn both German and Alemanic. He discovers German poetry especially the Romantic poets.
1925:	Baccalauréat in mathematics.
	Numerous unpublished notebooks already attest to his poet's vocation.
1926:	Unable, for financial reasons, to pursue higher education in Physics and chemistry as he wished, he prepares for the entrance exam to the Treasury by himself. At nineteen years old he is appointed deputy collector.
1930:	Promoted to the Rocroi treasury office, then to Mézières, he lives in Charleville (Rimbaud's birthplace).

1935: Selected by competitive exam he enters the general Direction office of the Board of Finance in Paris.

1937: A practicing catholic until then, he gradually abandons the Church during the Spanish Civil War. Meets Supervielle, becomes a close friend of Jean Follain. Numerous contacts with young poets.

1938: *Requiem*, first booklet of poems published by Tschann, Paris. From then on, will simulteanously pursue his career as a civil servant and a poet.

1939 Enlisted in the army in Besançon, meets Marcel Arland.

1942: First major publication *Terraqué, poèmes*, Gallimard, Paris.

Meets Paul Eluard.

1943: In the Resistance as Serpières, joins the clandestine communist party. In spite of long periods of questioning he will not leave it until 1980.

1944: Liberation of Paris. In the National Writers' Committee, stemming from the Résistance, Guillevic becomes acquainted with Aragon, Triolet, Tzara, Picasso and Léger . . . Meets Reverdy.

1945–47 Member of ministerial cabinets for National Economy and Reconstruction.

1946: Appointed National Economy Inspector.

1947: *Exécutoire*, *poèmes*, Gallimard.

1949: *Gagner, poèmes 1945–948*, Gallimard.

1951: *Terre à Bonheur,* Seghers.

1953–67: Summer holidays in Brittany, especially in Groix Island.

1954: *31 Sonnets*, prefaced by Louis Aragton, Gallimard.

1961: *Carnac, poème,* Gallimard.

1962: « Grand Prix du Mont St Michel »

1963: *Sphère, poèmes,* Gallimard.

1966: *Avec*, *poèmes*, Gallimard.

1967: *Euclidiennes, poèmes*, Gallimard.

Retires from his position as Inspector for National Economy.

1969: *Ville, poème*, Gallimard.

1970: *Paroi*, *poème,* Gallimard.

1971: *Encoches,* Editeurs Français Réunis.

1973: *Inclus, poème,* Gallimard.

1975: Revival of the Mallarmé Academy. Guillevic is elected as président. He will keep that responsibility until 1993.

1976: Grand Prix Bretagne.

Grand Prix de l'Académie Française.

Golden Crown awarded at the International Poetry Festival of Struga, Macedonia.

1977: *Du Domaine, poème,* Gallimard.

1979: *Etier, poèmes 1965–1975,* Gallimard.

1980: *Autres, poèmes, 1969–1979,* Gallimard.

1981: *Trouées, poèmes 1973–1980,* Gallimard.

1983: *Requis, poème 1977–1982,* Gallimard.

1984: Awarded the "Grand Prix National de Poésie."

1987: *Motifs, poèmes 1981–1984,* Gallimard.

Creusement, poèmes 1977–1986, Gallimard.

1989: *Art Poétique, poème 1985–1988,* Gallimard.

1990: *Le Chant, poème 1987–1988,* Gallimard.

1993: *Maintenant, poème 1986–1992,* Gallimard.

Guillevic & Jean Follain, en collaboration avec Lucie Albertini,

PAP, Pully, Suise.

1996: *Possibles futurs, poèmes 1982–1994,* Gallimard.

1997: The poet passes away at home in Paris on March 19.

2001: *Proses ou boire dans le secret des grottes,* edited by Lucie Albertini Guillevic and Jérôme Pelissier. Ed. Fischbacher, Paris, 2001.

2002: *Quotidiennes, poèmes 1994–1996.* Gallimard. Edited and introduced by L.A.G.

2003: *Guillevic, Choix de poèmes,* Gallimard jeunesse, Folio junior.

A selection of texts from 1924 to 1997. Edited and introduced by L.A.G.

2004: *Présent, poèmes 1987–1997,* Gallimard. Edited and introduced by L.A.G.

2006 *Lieux communs* suivi de *Van Gogh,* edited and introduced by Michael Brophy, Editions VVV, Halifax, Nova Scotia.

2007: *Relier, Poèmes 1938–1996*, Gallimard. Edited and introduced by L.A.G.

Translated into more than 50 languages in 60 countries, Guillevic was also the translator of Hölderlin, Heine, Goethe, Trakl, Rilke, Brecht and co-translated works from the Arabic, Finnish, Georgian, Hungarian, Italian, Macedonian, Russian, Roumanian, Swedish, Ukrainian, etc. He contributed to many anthologies including *Mes Poètes Hongrois,* Corvina, Budapest, 1967.

A board member of the "Société des gens de Lettres" into which he was received in 1942 by Paul Valéry. A member of the National Writer's Committee, The Pen Club, board member of the SACD, the SACEM, founding member of the Union of Writers and the "Maison des Ecrivains" and Honorary member of ATLF.

Guillevic was Commander of the Legion of Honor and Commander in the Order of Arts and Letters.

—MC and LAG

Selected Bibliography:

Paperback reprints, (not listed in the above chronology):
Terraqué, suivi de *Exécutoire*, Poésie Gallimard, Paris, 1968.
Sphère, suivi de *Carnac*, Poésie Gallimard, Paris, 1977.
Du domaine, *Euclidiennes*, Poésie Gallimard, 1985.
Etier, suivi de *Autres*, Poésie Gallimard, 2001.
Art poétique précédé de *Paroi* et suivi de *Le Chant*, Poésie Gallimard, 2005.
Possibles Futurs, Poésie Gallimard, 2007.

Critical bibliography:

Bowd, Gavin, *Guillevic, sauvage de la modernité*, University of Glasgow Press, French and German publications, Glasgow, 1992.

Brophy, Michael, *Eugène Guillevic*, Rodopi, Amsterdam, Atlanta, 1993.

Daix, Pierre, *Guillevic*, Collection Poètes d'aujourd'hui, Seghers, Paris, 1954.

Fetzer, Glenn W. "Eugène Guillevic, Of cosmos and the unbounded" and "The geometry connection" in *Palimpsests of the Real in Recent French Poetry,* pp55–84, Rodopi, Amsterdam, New York, 2004.

Fournier, Bernard, *Le cri du chat-huant, le lyrisme chez Guillevic*, L'Harmattan, 2002.

Gaubert, Serge (ed. by) *Lire Guillevic*, University Press of Lyon, 1983.

Harvey, Stella, *Myth and the Sacred in the Poetry of Guillevic*, Amsterdam, Rodopi, 1997.

Lopo, Maria, *Guillevic et sa Bretagne,* University Press of Rennes, Plurial 13, 2004.

Mitchell, Anne Marie, *Guillevic*, Le Temps parallèle Ed., Marseille, 1989

Pierrot Jean, *Guillevic ou la sérénité gagnée*, ed. Champ Vallon, coll. Champ poétique, 1984.

Rannou, Pascal, *Du Menhir au poème*, Skhol Vreizh, Morlaix, 1991.

Tortel, Jean, *Guillevic*, Collection Poètes d'Aujourd'hui, Seghers, Paris, 1962, 1971, 1978.

Winspur, Steven, *La poésie du lieu: Segalen, Thoreau, Guillevic, Ponge*, Rodopi, Amsterdam, New York, 2006.

Lectures de Guillevic. Approches critiques, Edited by par Sergio Villani, Paul Perron et Pascal Michelucci. Ed Legas, New York, Ottawa, Toronto, 2002

Guillevic ou la passion du monde. Textes réunis par Jacques Lardoux, University Press of Anger, 2003.

Interviews:

Vivre en poésie, with Lucie Albertini and Alain Vircondelet, Ed. Stock, Paris, 1980. Reprint, Paris, *Le temps des cerises*, 2007.

Choses parlées, Entretiens, Guillevic/Raymond Jean, Seyssell, Champ Vallon, 1982.

Guillevic/Jacques Lardoux, Humour-Terraqué, Entretiens lectures. University Press of Vincennes, 1997.

Guillevic, Un brin d'herbe après tout. Entretiens avec Jean Yves Erhel, La part commune, 1998.

Du pays de la pierre, entretiens entre Guillevic, Boris Lejeune et Lucie Albertini, Editions de la Différence, 2006.

Special issues:

Nu (e), edited by Enza Palamara et Béatrice Bonhomme, 2006.

Europe, edited by Bernard Fournier, 2007.

Works translated into English:

Guillevic, Selected Poems, Tr. Denise Levertov, New Directions, New York, 1968.

Guillevic, Tr. Teo Savory, Unicorn Press, Santa Barbara, 1968.

Selected Poems, Guillevic, Tr. and intr. by Teo Savory, Penguin Books, 1974.

Euclidians, Guillevic, Tr. Teo Savory, Unicorn Press, Greensboro, 1975.

Carnac, Tr. John Montague, Intr. Stephen Romer, Bloodaxe Books Ltd, Newcastle upon Tyne, 1999.

On Silence, Tr. Sergio Villani, Albion Press, Woodridge, Ontario, Canada, 1995.

Ne t'inquiète pas, Worry not. Tr. Joshua Watsky, with watercolours by Baltazar. Stonington, Wequetequock Cove, 1995.

Ciels du quotidien, bilingual edition with a translation by Joshua Watsky and illustrations by Bertemès, Baltazar and Olivier Debré. Paris, André Biren, May 1997.

Living in Poetry, Interview of Guillevic with Lucie Albertini and Alain Vircondelet. Tr. Maureen Smith, Dedalus Press, Dublin, 2002.

Time again / Encore le temps Tr. J. Watsky with lithographies by Baltazar. Ed Wequeliquock Cove, Newhaven, 2006.

Other works by Guillevic illustrated by Baltazar:

Eaux, manuscript poem, with washtint, Paris and Vitry, October 1986.
Cette lumière, with washtint, Nice, Jacques Matarasso, December 1987.
Tourbillon, with 12 engravings, Lyon, Ed. Alain Piroir, 1990.
Choix, manuscript poem with two washtints, 1990.
L'œil des pétales, manuscript poem with colour washtint, May 1991.
D'une lune, with lithographies, Paris, Ed. Biren, 1991.
Ne t'inquiète pas, manuscript poem with seven washtints, 1992.
L'infini, manuscript poem with two washtints, September 30, 1992.
Rêverie, Manuscript poem with one washtint, October 4, 1992.
L'orage, with four colour washtints, Stonington, Connecticut, Joshua Watsky Editions, 1993.
Plongées rituelles, with two engravings, Paris, Claude Blaizot, July 1995.
Exercice de conversation, Librairie Nicaise, Paris, December 1997.
Encore le temps, with engravings, Paris, Ed. Dumarchez, 2006.

—M.C. and L.A.G.

Patricia Terry was Professor of French Literature at Barnard College and the University of California San Diego until her retirement in 1991. Among her verse translations are *Poems of Jules Laforgue, The Song of Roland, Poems of the Elder Edda, The Honeysuckle and the Hazel Tree, Renard the Fox,* and *Roof Slates and Other Poems of Pierre Reverdy* (with Mary Ann Caws). Recent titles include *Capital of Pain* by Paul Eluard (with Mary Ann Caws & Nancy Kline), an illustrated edition of *Lancelot and the Lord of the Distant Isles: Or, The Book of Galehaut Retold* (with Samuel N. Rosenberg), and a book of her own poems, *Words of Silence.* At present she is working on a new revised and much expanded edition of the *Poems of Jules Laforgue* (to be published by Black Widow Press in 2008) and, with Samuel N. Rosenberg, on a collection of late medieval folk poems from France and Spain.

Monique Chefdor was Professor of French and Comparative Literature at Scripps College, Claremont University Center, California. She has also taught in Southern Rhodesia (now Zimbabwe); the Universities of Exeter, England; Rochester, NY; Sarah Lawrence College, NY; Hollins College, Virginia; and the University of Picardie Jules Vernes, Amiens, France. She is the author of several books and articles on Blaise Cendrars, Chirico, Proust, and Segalen. She has written much on the the relationship between writers and painters, including contributing to the recent creation of a DVD on Guillevic and painters produced by the University of Rennes, France. She established the bibliography of Guillevic's works illustrated by artists and was selected to write the notice on Guillevic published by the French Board of Culture in the brochure of the 2007 Célébrations Nationales.

All Black Widow Press titles are printed on acid-free paper and bound into a sewn and glued binding. Manufactured in the United States of America.

www.blackwidowpress.com

This book was set in Simoncini Garamond. The titling font is Aculida, a modernistic typeface used by many of the Dadaists in their typographic artworks.

typeset & designed by Windhaven Press
www.windhaven.com

green press INITIATIVE

Black Widow Press is committed to preserving ancient forests and natural resources. We elected to print *The Sea And Other Poems* on 50% post consumer recycled paper, processed chlorine free. As a result, for this printing, we have saved:

18 Trees (40' tall and 6-8" diameter)
7,498 Gallons of Wastewater
3,016 Kilowatt Hours of Electricity
826 Pounds of Solid Waste
1,624 Pounds of Greenhouse Gases

Black Widow Press made this paper choice because our printer, Thomson-Shore, Inc., is a member of Green Press Initiative, a nonprofit program dedicated to supporting authors, publishers, and suppliers in their efforts to reduce their use of fiber obtained from endangered forests.

For more information, visit www.greenpressinitiative.org